SPORTS FOR ALL

Other Books by Author

Simply Notetaking (forthcoming)
Skill Building for ESL and Special Education: Student Textbook (2016)
Skill Building for ESL and Special Education: Student Workbook (2016)
Skill Building for ESL and Special Education: Teacher's Text (2016)
The Eight Parts of Speech: Student Text and Workbook (2017)
The Eight Parts of Speech: Teacher's Text (2017)

SPORTS FOR ALL

Creating an Intramural Sports Program for Middle and High School Students

Kristine Setting Clark

Rowman & Littlefield
Lanham • Boulder • New York • London

All bracket diagrams are used courtesy of PrintyourBrackets.com, while all sports layout diagrams are used courtesy of sportsknowhow.com.

Published by Rowman & Littlefield
An imprint of The Rowman & Littlefield Publishing Group, Inc.
4501 Forbes Boulevard, Suite 200, Lanham, Maryland 20706
www.rowman.com

6 Tinworth Street, London SE11 5AL, United Kingdom

Copyright © 2019 by Kristine Setting Clark

All rights reserved. No part of this book may be reproduced in any form or by any electronic or mechanical means, including information storage and retrieval systems, without written permission from the publisher, except by a reviewer who may quote passages in a review.

British Library Cataloguing in Publication Information Available

Library of Congress Cataloging-in-Publication Data Available

ISBN 9781475851526 (pbk.)
ISBN 9781475851533 (electronic)

Contents

Mission Statement	vii
Introduction	ix
1 Why a Sports for All Intramural Program?	1
2 Getting Started: Designing Your School's Sports for All Intramural Program	3
3 Organization of the Intramural Program	5
4 Programming and Scheduling	7
5 Officials, Sportsmanship, Health, and Safety	11
6 Promotions: Getting the Word Out!	15
7 Intramural Sports and Activities	19
8 Awards	61
9 Evaluation and Assessment	63
10 In Summary	67
Appendix: Sports for All Program Forms and Templates	69
References	117
About the Author	119

Mission Statement

Sports for All Intramural Sports Program

The mission of the Sports for All intramural sports program is to create added experiences for the school's growth and development by encouraging involvement in the present, which will enrich and challenge the future. Competitive and recreational athletics are an integral part of the educational process and experience. Students should have the opportunity to participate and compete as appropriate to their interests and skills.

Intramurals provide cocurricular value by contributing to overall community satisfaction, involvement, and learning within a diverse setting, improving student recruitment and retention by adding to the quality of community life and creating a venue for social interaction, integration, and leadership activities, which positively affect spirit, mind, and body.

As physical educators, we value the lessons that have long been taught by athletic participation: the pursuit of excellence through personal development and teamwork; ethical and responsible behavior on the field and off; adherence to the spirit of rules and to their letter; leadership and strength of character; and sportsmanship, including respect for one's opponents, acceptance of victory with humility, and acknowledgment of defeat with grace.

In teaching these lessons to students, the Sports for All intramural program instills habits that lead students to better and healthier lives. While winning is not an end in itself, we believe that the efforts by our intramural and intermural teams to be their best will lead them to success. Athletic participation is a way for students to grow and learn and enjoy themselves and to use and develop their personal, physical, and intellectual skills. The entire sports and athletic departments, including coaches, medical and training staff, facilities and equipment personnel, and administrators, work to achieve these goals, honor the values of the school, and support the principles of the Sports for All intramural program.

Physical educators believe that a comprehensive athletics program provides physical, social, and emotional benefits that are vitally important in a highly competitive educational environment. Since the number of students who can compete on school athletic teams is limited, an extensive program of intramural sports should be developed.

Values of the Sports for All Intramural Program

1. Great opportunity for student leadership
2. Introduces students to a wide variety of activities
3. Far less expensive to administer than other programs
4. Little expenditure for equipment
5. Natural extension and outgrowth of the physical education program
6. Allows for maximum use of facilities
7. Minimal (expense) yet meaningful recognition awards
8. Program can be eligible for grants and support from public and private foundations
9. Certificated, trained, and qualified staff already available for each school
10. Can involve retired teachers and coaches for consultation

Introduction

The department of sports and athletics should be committed to providing a Sports for All intramural sports program.

The mission of Sports for All is to create added experiences for the school's growth and development by encouraging involvement in the present, which will enrich and challenge the future.

Competitive and recreational athletics are an integral part of the educational process and experience. Students should have the opportunity to participate and compete as appropriate to their interest and skill.

Intramurals provide cocurricular value by contributing to overall community satisfaction, involvement, and learning within a diverse setting, improving student recruitment and retention by adding to the quality of community life and creating a venue for social interaction, integration, and leadership activities, which positively affect spirit, mind, and body.

As physical educators, we value the lessons that have long been taught by athletic participation: the pursuit of excellence through personal development and teamwork; ethical and responsible behavior on the field and off; adherence to the spirit of rules and to their letter; leadership and strength of character; and sportsmanship, including respect for one's opponents, acceptance of victory with humility, and acknowledgment of defeat with grace.

In teaching these lessons to students, the Sports for All program will instill habits that will lead students to better and healthier lives. While winning is not an end in itself, we believe that the efforts by our intramural and intermural teams to be their best will lead them to success.

Athletic participation is a way for students to grow and learn and to use and develop their personal, physical, and intellectual skills. The entire physical education and athletic departments, including coaches, medical and training staff, facilities and equipment personnel, and administrators, work to achieve these goals, honor the values of the school, and support the principles of the Sports for All intramural program.

Physical educators believe that a comprehensive athletic program provides physical, social, and emotional benefits that are vitally important in a highly competitive educational environment. Competition, in itself, is a dynamic that plays a vital role in life and is imperative to success.

Since the number of students who can compete at the athletic team level is limited, each school should develop an extensive intramural sports program. Let Sports for All be that program!

Author's Note: Your school's Sports for All intramural program can be as elaborate or as simple as you choose. The main emphasis of the program is that the participants have fun, gain knowledge from their experiences, and learn the art of good sportsmanship.

1

Why a Sports for All Intramural Program?

At a time when our country is struggling with a widespread obesity problem, physical activity couldn't be more important for our nation's health. Intramural sports programs provide a great opportunity for those who don't have the athletic caliber of skill to compete in school sports.

The Sports for All intramural sports program focuses on modifying and expanding many of the existing curriculum activities and games in middle school and high school as a way to motivate students by making physical education/intramural sports interesting and fun as they are learning. This program has also been developed to invoke success, self-confidence, and enthusiasm for each and every student within each activity *regardless* of athletic ability. Many of the tournament formats, activities, activity variations, and assessments are unique.

Although tests of muscular and cardiovascular endurance, strength, power, hand-eye coordination, flexibility, and agility were important considerations, other factors also influenced the selection of events used in intramurals. The physical movements and skill items had to be common enough to be found in most physical education programs. The equipment used for each event had to be standard items found in most public middle and high schools. It was also necessary to simplify the structure, measurement, and scoring system. Finally, each event was designed to be fun for the participant as well as adaptable to spectator interest. Intramural sports are and have always been a way for students to discover their own latent talents, not to mention a prime source for discovering new talent for athletic teams.

Activity Variations

The activity variations encompass a wide range of activities and interests, be they individual, team, gender, grade, class, or mixed. Each game and activity should list its objectives, essentials/equipment needed, how to play, student tasks, and variations that will challenge the students at any secondary level. Safety is always a concern and should be covered in a conscientious manner before any activity or game begins.

All activities should include additional safety precautions when necessary. You may alter any activity to fit the needs, interests, and skills of each grade level. Easy-to-read diagrams, student forms, and layouts will be provided for most activities. All forms and information can be copied, placed on a clipboard, and used during intramural activity time.

Tournaments

Team scheduling, single and multiple schedules, formats, and rotation forms will enhance the organizational aspects of grouping students for intramural play. All forms can be found in the appendix to this book and can be easily copied and used year after year.

Evaluation and Assessments

At the end of the year, each school will have the chance to assess its own Sports for All intramural program. Assessment forms have been made available to you in the appendix to this book.

It is my hope that this program will allow participants to explore both physical education and intramurals, experience a wide variety of activities, set individual goals, enjoy more opportunities for success, and benefit from sports' many lifelong resources.

2

Getting Started: Designing Your School's Sports for All Intramural Program

Before you decide to implement an intramural sports program at your school, there is a detailed to-do list that needs to be followed and established prior to the creation of your program.

You will need to complete the following eight steps in the order presented:

1. Meet with your athletic director, physical education instructors, coaches, and anyone else who may be involved with sports and athletics to discuss your proposed program.
2. Present a program outline to your administrative staff with a mission statement, structure of program, goals, objectives, evaluations and assessments, budget, leadership roles, rules and regulations, sign-ups, parental release forms, personnel required, publicity/promotions, parental and community involvement, entry requirements, awards and integration, and support from other school academic departments.
3. Speak to your administrators about making your intramural sports program part of your daily work load. In other words, you may request an additional prep period for work on the intramural program.
4. Check with parents and the community for volunteer help and support with the program.
5. Create and develop an intramural sports council. Positions can be filled in later once you get authorization to continue with the project.
6. Survey the students regarding which sports they would like to be included in the intramural sports program.
7. Meet a second time with your athletic director, physical education instructors, coaches, and anyone else who may be involved with sports and athletics to make any changes and finalize the proposal.
8. After getting the final approval from your administrative staff to proceed with the project, inform the students and the faculty and begin your publicity for the program.

On the next page is a sample Sports for All intramural sports council chart. This will help you to get started on creating your program.

Table 2.1. Sports for All—Intramural Sports Council

Director of Athletics				
Intramural Sports Director				
Intramural Council Director, Physical Education Department/Coaches/Faculty 6 Student Body Members (3 boys and 3 girls)				
Activities, Rules, and Regulations Committee 3–4 Council Members		Facility Scheduling and Statistics Committee 3–4 Council Members		Participant Selection Committee 3–4 Council Members
Officiating Committee	Equipment Managers		Promotions Committee	Awards Committee
Participants				
Student Body				

3

Organization of the Intramural Program

The key to a great intramural program is a great intramural council. Granted, the administration and faculty are needed to get the program off the ground, but it is the intramural council who helps lead and implement the intramural program under the direction of the intramural director. Below is a breakdown of the various positions and committees.

Director of Athletics

The director of athletics will have oversight of all intramural policies and activities and may change or suspend intramural activities at any time with or without notice. The director of athletics will also be responsible for selecting the intramural sports director.

Intramural Sports Director

The intramural sports director will have oversight of all intramural policies and activities, including the selection of the intramural council. The intramural sports director will be responsible for supervising the activities of the intramural council.

Intramural Council

The intramural council will be responsible for administering and implementing the intramural program. It will also oversee and coordinate all committees.

Activities, Rules, and Regulations Committee

The activities, rules, and regulations committee will be responsible for which activities will be offered. The committee will also oversee the officiating committee and determine rules and regulations as well as establish and enforce rules on eligibility, participation, sportsmanship, and protests. The committee will also be responsible for setting up spectator rules and regulations.

Facility Scheduling and Statistics Committee

The facility scheduling and statistics committee will be responsible for scheduling *all* intramural events. This will include the day, date, time, and location of facility. This committee will also record all stats of each and every game, including but not limited to results, standings, and scores. The statistics committee will work closely with the promotions and public relations committee to keep all scores and other information up to date on posters and daily announcements.

Participant Selection Committee

The participant selection committee is responsible for the equalization of competition in teams on the basis of skill. Since this is intramurals and *not* athletics, each student who is assigned to a team will be given equal playing time *regardless* of skill level.

Officiating Committee

The officiating committee is responsible for recruiting all referees, umpires, scorekeepers, timekeepers, and linesmen. All officials' schedules will be posted in advance with the activity, day, date, time, and facility. All officials will notify the team captains of any and all rule changes. Be sure to reiterate to *all* participants that the referee is *always* right. Due to the time constraint on all activities, there will be no time for instant replays.

Equipment Managers

The equipment managers are responsible for the set-up of all equipment *prior* to the event. Following the end of each event, the managers must be sure to return all equipment and report any broken or damaged equipment to the activities council. There should be at least two or three managers at each event.

Promotions Committee

The promotions committee will be responsible for publicizing all facets of the intramural program, from sign-ups to final game scores. Emphasis should be placed on equal participation for *all*. This will attract the nonathlete. There should also be a notice board *solely* for intramurals. The committee will also recruit videographers, photographers to take action and team photos, and journalism class reporters to report the sports news of the day. It is imperative that the committee post all game results by the following day, whether on a wall, through school announcements, or by email. Include your intramural sports program on the school's website. Post scores, information, photos, videos, and team and individual player performances.

Awards Committee

The awards committee is at the mercy of the money allotted to the intramural program. The committee can also recruit funds from the community. A school awards assembly would also be the responsibility of the awards committee and would be a great way to end each semester.

4
Programming and Scheduling

Programming

The caliber of an intramural program is highly dependent on the imagination and creativity of its leadership.

Other than being limited in participating on a school athletic team, there are three factors that distinguish an intramural program from athletics:

1. Intramural activities are completely voluntary in nature. The student has a choice of activities to choose from.
2. Every student is given an *equal opportunity* to participate regardless of physical ability.
3. Students have the opportunity to be involved in the planning, organization, and administration of programs. It is imperative that such involvement is always under the supervision and guidance of the intramural director.

Sports for All Objectives and Goals

1. Provide an opportunity to participate in sports activities without regard for high performance skill or ability.
2. Provide activities in a safe and professionally supervised area.
3. Foster healthy competition, sportsmanship, and team unity.
4. Develop a sense of community within the school.
5. Enhance social interaction.
6. Expose students to a healthy lifestyle of physical fitness.

So whether it be for middle school or high school, an intramural sports program needs to be balanced and provide equal opportunity for all students. The major differences between middle school and high school are age, physical development, fitness level, and physical and mental maturity of students. These five factors will determine which activities you will include in your school's intramural program.

Your program must also include special education students. Inclusion is a major part of intramural sports, and there is no better way than to include these students in as many activities and teams as possible.

The three factors that are a must for any successful intramural sports program are (1) a variety of activities, (2) team and individual sports activities, and (3) a schedule of tournament play.

Choosing Your Program's Activities

The following are important points that should be considered by the activities, rules, and regulations committee prior to deciding on a list of activities:

1. Select activities based on your facilities, equipment, and the seasons.
2. Select activities that are most interesting to the students. Give them a list of activities, and allow them to add alternative activities that they are interested in. Remember, though, it must be a physical activity.
3. Be sure to incorporate a few less skilled activities. Instead of emphasizing competition, focus on making the activities enjoyable.
4. Outside of the more highly skilled activities, you may want to present the sport in a progressive manner. For instance, if an unskilled student is interested in playing team basketball, suggest modified basketball games such as HORSE or Around the World for starters.
5. Physical education class sports can be filtered into your intramural sports program.
6. Depending on your grade level, promote coed activities.
7. Create a timeline for your activities.

Scheduling

The successful intramural program will implement the greatest amount of intramural time with as many activities as possible with as many students as possible.

The facility scheduling and statistics committee is responsible for the scheduling and statistics data for all activities. There are many scheduling models to choose from, but you want to keep this as simple as possible. Below are the three basic models that I feel will work best with the middle and high school levels.

Round Robin—Single Elimination

This is, by far, the best (and simplest) model for all activities. Each team plays every team once in their given activity. Once a team has lost, they are eliminated from further play. The team who remains undefeated throughout the tournament is the champion. This works well with large school intramural programs.

Round Robin—Double Elimination

Each team plays every team once in their given activity but is not eliminated until they have lost twice. Once again, the team who remains undefeated throughout the tournament is the champion. This works well with small school intramural programs. It can be extremely time consuming.

Consolation Bracket

This consolation tournament is for all the players who were eliminated in the first round robin—single elimination. You can also do the same with the players who were eliminated in the round robin—double elimination.

Always remember to schedule around holidays. In regard to tournaments, it is imperative that you properly schedule seeded teams/individual teams and byes accordingly.

Team and Individual Sports Scheduling

You may want to refer to this scheduling when playing a round robin tournament. Scheduling an even number of teams will not be a problem, but when scheduling an odd number of teams there will always be one team out. Team X will have a bye for that day/week and will be rotated in accordingly. See the example below:

4 Teams

1-2	1-4	1-3
4-3	3-2	2-4

5 Teams

1-2	5-1	4-5	3-4	2-3
5-3	4-2	3-1	2-5	1-4
X-4	X-3	X-2	X-1	X-5

6 Teams

1-2	1-6	1-5	1-4	1-3
6-3	5-2	4-6	3-5	2-4
5-4	4-3	3-2	2-6	6-5

7 Teams

1-2	7-1	6-7	5-6	4-5	3-4	2-3
7-3	6-2	5-1	4-7	3-6	2-5	1-4
6-4	5-3	4-2	3-1	2-7	1-6	7-5
X-5	X-4	X-3	X-2	X-1	X-7	X-6

8 Team

1-2	1-8	1-7	1-6	1-5	1-4	1-3
8-3	7-2	6-8	5-7	4-6	3-5	2-4
7-4	6-3	5-2	4-8	3-7	2-6	8-5
6-5	5-4	4-3	3-2	2-8	8-7	7-6

9 Teams

1-2	9-1	8-9	7-8	6-7	5-6	4-5	3-4	2-3
9-3	8-2	7-1	6-9	5-8	4-7	3-6	2-5	1-4
8-4	7-3	6-2	5-1	4-9	3-8	2-7	1-6	9-5
7-5	6-4	5-3	4-2	3-1	2-9	1-8	9-7	8-6
X-6	X-5	X-4	X-3	X-2	X-1	X-9	X-8	X-7

10 Teams

1-2	1-10	1-9	1-8	1-7	1-6	1-5	1-4	1-3	
10-3	9-2	8-10	7-9	6-8	5-7	4-6	3-5	2-4	
9-4	8-3	7-2	6-10	5-9	4-8	3-7	2-6	10-5	
8-5	7-4	6-3	5-2	4-10	3-9	2-8	10-7	9-6	
7-6	6-5	5-4	4-3	3-2	2-10	10-9	9-8	8-7	

5
Officials, Sportsmanship, Health, and Safety

Officials

Umpires, referees, timekeepers, scorekeepers, and other intramural sports officials will preside over intramural sporting events to help maintain standards of play. They identify infractions and implement penalties according to the rules of the game.

Since the intramurals will be played at the middle and/or high school level, it would be ideal if the umpires and referees were pooled from the school's faculty, but this is not always possible. If this is the case, you may want to incorporate students who are knowledgeable about the game, fair, and reliable to help in officiating games.

Officials, whether faculty or students, should know the rules of the game and be confident and decisive in their decision making.

Duties and Responsibilities of the Officiating Team

1. Preside over and officiate intramural sporting events and competitions.
2. Judge performances to determine a winner.
3. Inspect equipment, and examine all participants to ensure safety. (Players should not wear jewelry or have open cuts or sores.)
4. Know the event times, and start and stop play when necessary.
5. Enforce the rules of the game, and assess penalties when necessary.
6. Signal participants and other officials when infractions occur.
7. Settle claims of infractions by participants, but at this level there is no instant replay; therefore, the officials' call is not up for debate.
8. While officiating, it is imperative that the officiating staff strategically position themselves on the field, court, or playing space where they can best see the action, assess the situation, and identify any violation of the rules.
9. Make sure that all officials have whistles.

Duties and Responsibilities of the Scorekeeper and Timekeeper

Scorekeeper

1. Pick up pencils, clipboard, and rosters from the intramural office.
2. Before each game the scorekeeper should have a roster of each team. Each player should be identified by name. If the players are wearing jerseys, numbers, or pinnies, each participant should be identified by his or her number.
3. Keep track of substitutions.
4. Keep track of individual and team fouls, warnings, and ejections. Alert the referee when a player is in foul trouble.
5. Know signs and abbreviations for penalties and fouls.
6. Ensure that game sheets are completed correctly and that all copies are readable before getting the referee to sign them at the end of the game.
7. Ensure that each team is given a copy of the game sheet after it is signed by the referee.
8. Check frequently with the timekeeper to make sure the score in the book is the same as the score on the clock.

Timekeeper

1. Set the clock at the beginning of each game according to that game's rules with the correct amount of time. Also have a stopwatch on hand if needed.
2. Keep score on the clock for each team during the game.
3. Indicate the appropriate quarter for the game.
4. If possible, indicate the direction of the next alternate possession; the arrow corresponds to the direction the team is going.
5. Set the clock for three minutes at halftime and let it run. The referee may shorten halftime if behind schedule.
6. Start and stop the clock as indicated by the referee. The clock should stop any time the timekeeper hears a referee's whistle and at no other time.
7. Immediately get the referee's attention if you have any questions or problems with the clock.
8. Check frequently with the scorekeeper to make sure that the score on the clock is the same as the score in the book.

Intramural sports officials rely on their judgment to rule on infractions and penalties. These rulings sometimes result in strong disagreement expressed by players and/or spectators. It is extremely important that the players and spectators know that arguments and harassment of the officials will result in the player being ejected and the spectators being removed.

Sportsmanship

Over the past decade, we have seen more unsportsmanlike conduct in professional sports than ever before. What's worse is that it has trickled down to the K–12 age groups as they emulate their professional sports heroes. Taunting, talking trash, and taking cheap shots along with team or individual victory celebrations are all too common in the world of sports.

This type of behavior is the exact opposite of the definition of sportsmanship. These actions can lead to a penalty, which, in turn, can cost players the game.

The Five Major Components of Sportsmanship

1. Playing fair
2. Obeying the rules and regulations of the game
3. Exhibiting self-control at all times
4. Respecting the decisions of the officials
5. Treating everyone, including opponents, with respect

Practicing Good Sportsmanship

1. Know your sport, and play by the rules. Attend practice on time, play to the best of your ability, and support the other players on the team.
2. Show courtesy and respect for everyone involved in the game (before, during, and after); that includes the players on both teams and the officials.
3. Never lose your temper. It only makes matters worse.
4. Do not, under any circumstances, settle arguments or disputes with violence. Contact a faculty member immediately.
5. Officials are human and do make mistakes, but, in sports, the official call is usually the *only* call that matters. Accept and respect their decisions.
6. Win or lose, show some class by congratulating your opponent on a game well played.

The importance of winning should never become so overriding that players lose sight of appropriate behavior. The playing field is not a venue for physical or verbal abuse by the players or spectators. Failure to display an acceptable degree of sportsmanship will render a participant ineligible for further participation in any intramural sport or activity. These decisions lie solely with the intramural sports director.

The conduct of all players before and after the game is as important as conduct during the game.

Health and Safety

One of the main goals of a successful intramural program is to improve the health and safety of the participants. The following steps are critical in achieving this goal:

1. All activities will be structured to ensure that all safety requirements are met.
2. Each and every student will have a medical clearance prior to participation. This information is available through the student's counselor. Be sure to check the dates of the last medical clearance. To reiterate, Sports for All intramural sports permission letters *need* to be on file!
3. Appropriate clothing and shoes will be worn at all times. No jewelry will be allowed to be worn during game play.
4. Locker rooms will be supervised to ensure safety.
5. Supervision will be present at *all* intramural sport and game events to ensure safety as well as progression of the event.
6. Due to the physical nature of the events, injuries can and will occur. Parental consent and permission forms need to be on file before any participant can play. First aid kits must be available for all events. Plans for communication with emergency services need to be in place, and all staff must follow emergency procedures.

Facilities and Equipment

Regardless of your district's budget, adequate facilities and equipment is imperative, not to mention crucial to a successful intramural sports program. If your school does not have a state-of-the-art gym facility or top-of-the-line equipment, it should not deter you from having a thriving and effective program. Activities can be modified to meet your budget and the space available.

The three basic guidelines to follow are as follows:

1. The facilities should be sufficient to meet the needs, interests, safety, and number of student participants.
2. If possible, the equipment used for intramural sports should be separate from the equipment used by the physical education department. I know that for many of you this is not feasible. Even though much of the equipment can be shared, each program needs its own separate budget.
3. Maintenance for both facilities and equipment is essential for both health and safety reasons.

6

Promotions: Getting the Word Out!

Promotions Committee

The promotions committee will be responsible for publicizing all facets of the Sports for All intramural program, from sign-ups to final game scores. Emphasis should be placed on equal participation for *all*.

School Website

In an age of technology, the promotions committee should promote the intramural program on the school's website. With students (and parents) having access to smartphones, computers, tablets, and so on, the Internet would be the best way to get the word out.

Develop an Email Newsletter

Email is a great way to keep students, parents, and fans informed of upcoming events.

Social Media

Students are one of the largest groups on social media today. Almost everyone is affiliated with at least one platform, such as Facebook, Twitter, YouTube, Instagram, and so on. The majority of these networks are free and, therefore, perfect for school advertising. It's an ideal venue for receiving important information and updates on game results, images, and videos from the various games and competitions.

Although social media is an excellent tool for promoting your Sports for All intramural program, don't downplay the *traditional* method of advertising.

The Oldest Method of Communication—Word of Mouth

Word of mouth is the most common method of communication. Students will talk about the program with friends, and they, in turn, will talk about it with their friends, and so the message gets out. But in order for this method to be successful, you need to keep everyone informed by alternative advertising.

Paper Promotions: Posters, Banners, Bulletin Boards, and Flyers

Use simple and creative ways to promote your program. Posters, banners, and flyers are a great way to include the computer department in your intramural sports program. With today's technology, they have the tools to create professional advertisements and display them throughout the school. It may also be possible for the computer class instructor to assign projects as class assignments.

Bulletin Boards and PA Systems

There should also be a bulletin board solely for intramurals strategically placed within the school premises so that all students will be able to read the game scores and updates.

The school's PA system is a great way to promote the program. It will allow for each and every student, faculty member, and staff to hear the latest information regarding the intramural program.

Integration and Support from Other Subject Areas

This is an extremely important facet in coordinating the Sports for All intramural program. By incorporating the entire school, everyone will feel that they are an important part of the program. All subject areas can show their support and spirit by displaying their work on the walls outside of their classrooms or in hallway displays. Below are some other ideas on how to integrate the Sports for All intramural program with the rest of the school.

Art Department

Like the computer department, the art department can contribute by drawing original posters and possibly even creating awards (i.e., ceramics).

Industrial Arts

The industrial arts class could be responsible for creating trophies and help in the construction of certain activities, such as obstacle courses that require their assistance.

Journalism and Photography (Photography Club)

Journalism students can be utilized to report the sports news of the day, while photography students could be recruited as photographers and videographers. They would be responsible for individual and team photos as well as action shots and recording the various activities. The work of both the journalism and the photography departments could be found in the school newspaper, social media, YouTube, and the school's website.

Health Department

Students can write on improving the quality of life through active lifestyles and the interactive roles of components such as physical exercise, stress, rest, personal hygiene, nutrition, and substance abuse in determining personal health and wellness. Emphasis could be placed on learning about peaceful conflict resolution and developing effective coping skills, all of which are necessary for positive social interaction. Some of these compositions could even be published on the intermural website.

Mathematics Department

The math department could be responsible for all stats coverage of all events. Students could also calculate probabilities and create graphs to demonstrate measurements and comparisons of the teams' and participants' progress.

Music Department

The music department would be responsible for the entertainment at the events. They could possibly create certain music for certain events.

Science Department

The science department can incorporate biomechanics and kinesiology by being on site to monitor blood pressure and conduct pulse checks for fitness analysis of the participants.

Social Studies and History Department

Students could write on the history of sports as a class project or for the school newspaper, website, or hall displays. They could also map out a cross-country course for an event if needed.

Foreign Language Department

Students could write or give a presentation on an account of the week's events in various languages. This would also be a way of promoting cross-cultural understanding and acceptance. Some of the compositions could be viewed as hall displays or published on the website. The presentations could be recorded and presented on the website.

Computer Department

The computer department could work closely with the other departments. Students can use software to create lifestyle profiles and databases, analyze activity patterns, and reinforce exercise physiology concepts.

7

Intramural Sports and Activities

The following is a list of many of the more popular sports and activities that can be offered in the Sports for All intramural sports program. It is by no means a complete and comprehensive guide, but included are those activities that students most often want to do. Each of the activities can be changed, altered, or modified to fit the age/grade of the competitors. Instructors have the freedom to create and conjure up new ideas and methods that will further challenge students and enhance student success. All faculty should be enterprising, resourceful, and imaginative. Do not be afraid to listen to the students; they often have great new ideas because of their lack of a fixed mindset.

It is my hope that student interest and participation is enhanced since the same activities can be changed to add variety and excitement. Our goal is to get every student involved in the Sports for All intramural program. Let's bring back the individual and school spirit, praise, and esteem that once stood so strong in years past. Together, we can make that dream a reality.

Table 7.1. List of Intramural Sports and Activities

Individual—Team—Mixed—Grade vs. Grade—Class vs. Class	
Sport	**Activity**
Aerobics	Aerobic Dance
	Step Aerobics
Aquatics	Swimming/Diving Events
	Water Polo
Badminton	Individual and Team
Baseball	Fast Pitch and/or Slow Pitch
Basketball	5-Player Team Games
	Around the World
	Slam Dunk Hoops
	HORSE
	Hunch
	3-Point Shooting for Time
	Free-Throw Shooting from Key for Time
Cross Country (Short and Long Course)	Individual and Team
Fitness Testing	Softball Throw for Distance
	40-Yard Dash
	50-Yard Dash
	100-Yard Dash
	Mile Run
	Standing Broad/Long Jump
	Running Long Jump
	Sit-Ups
	Push-Ups
	Pull-Ups
	Shuttle Run
	Vertical Reach
	Sit and Reach
Football	7-Player Flag Football Teams
	Passing for Distance
	Passing for Accuracy
	Punting for Distance
	Kicking Field Goals for Distance
Frisbee	7-Player Frisbee Flag Football
Hockey	Floor Hockey Teams (Outdoors)
	Sock Hockey Teams (Indoors)

Horseshoes	Individual and Team
Obstacle Course	Designing Your Own Course (be creative!)
Soccer	11-Player Teams
Softball	Fast Pitch and/or Slow Pitch
Table Tennis	Individual and Team
Tennis	Individual and Team
Track and Field: Modified Decathlon	40-Yard Dash
	50-Yard Dash
	100-Yard Dash
	Mile Run
	Standing Broad/Long Jump
	Running Long Jump
	High Jump
	Shot Put
	Discus Throw
	400-Yard Team Relay
Volleyball	6-Player Teams

Aerobics: Aerobic Dance

Objective

To improve cardiovascular health, coordination, flexibility, and strength.

Facility and Equipment

- Gymnasium or school dance studio
- Great music to exercise
- Stopwatch or watch with second hand for pulse count
- Sign-up sheets

How to Perform the Activity

1. Start the music!
2. Begin with marching in place to warm up.
3. Swing your arms back and forth as you march.
4. Follow the instructor as she or he leads you into an aerobic dance routine.
5. Create a variation of arm movements, kicks, hops, and jumps without stopping for a minimum of 20 minutes.

Variations

1. Change the tempo of the music to slower or faster depending on the caliber of your participants.
2. Over time, increase the intensity of the moves.

Safety

- Be sure that students are far enough apart so that they can't hit or kick each other during the exercise.

Aerobics: Step Aerobics

Objective

To improve cardiovascular health, coordination, flexibility, and strength.

Facility and Equipment

- Gymnasium or school dance studio
- Aerobic dance steps with optional step heights
- Great music to exercise
- Stopwatch or watch with second hand for pulse count
- Sign-up sheets

How to Perform the Activity

1. Set height of your step to what is comfortable for you. Beginners should start at the lowest level.
2. Start the music!
3. Begin with marching in place to warm up.
4. Swing your arms back and forth as you march.
5. Follow the instructor as he or she leads you into a step aerobic routine. Create a variation of arm movements, kicks, hops, and jumps without stopping for a minimum of 20 minutes.

Variations

1. Change the tempo of the music to slower or faster depending on the caliber of your participants.
2. Over time, increase the intensity of the moves.

Safety

- Be sure that students are far enough apart so that they can't hit or kick each other during the exercise.
- Be sure that the steps are on an even surface.
- Always begin a step aerobic workout with a 10-minute warm-up.

Aquatics: Swimming/Diving Events

Objective

To develop endurance, skill, and conditioning in various swimming/diving event competitions and to be faster than your opponents.

Facility and Equipment

- School swimming pool or public swimming pool
- 1-meter and/or 3-meter diving board for diving events
- Swim caps (optional)
- Stopwatches
- Referees/whistles
- Scorekeepers
- Individual and team rosters

How to Perform the Activity

1. You may not have the participants and/or the skill to include all the events listed below. Choose from the following swimming events the ones that will work best for your program according to the skill caliber of your participants:
   - 50-yard freestyle
   - 100-yard freestyle
   - 200-yard freestyle
   - 50-yard breaststroke
   - 100-yard breaststroke
   - 200-yard breaststroke
   - 50-yard backstroke
   - 100-yard backstroke
   - 200-yard backstroke
   - 50-yard butterfly
   - 100-yard butterfly
   - 200-yard butterfly
   - 100-yard individual medley
   - 100-yard medley relay
   - 200-yard individual medley
   - 200-yard medley relay
2. Set up heats for each event.
3. Be sure to incorporate the diving competition halfway through the swimming events.
4. The caliber of the diving participants will determine which dives will be performed. Depending on the facility, you will have a choice of using the 1-meter board and/or the 3-meter board.

Variations

1. Change the distances of the events.

Safety

- No running, no glass objects, and no food are permitted in and around the pool area.

Aquatics: Water Polo

Objective

To score the most points by throwing the ball through the opposing team's goal and to defend their own goal from being scored on by the opposing team.

Facility and Equipment

- School swimming pool or public swimming pool
- Numbered protective head gear
- Referee/whistle
- Scorekeeper/scorebook
- Timekeeper/stopwatch
- Team rosters
- Coin for coin flip

How to Play the Game

1. There are 7 players per team: 1 goalie and 6 field players. One team will wear a dark-colored cap (normally blue) while the other will wear a light-colored cap (normally white). Each team can only have 7 players in the water at one time.
2. A water polo game is broken up into 4 quarters, each lasting 7 minutes. Each quarter begins with a sprint for the ball.
3. The referee will blow the whistle to start the period, and 1 player from each team will race to get the ball, which is floating at center pool. The winner of the sprint will control the ball on offense.
4. The offense has a 35-second shot clock to attempt to score. During that time, referees will call fouls against the players in the water for rule violations.
5. The game continues in motion until a goal is scored. After a goal is scored, both teams return to their defending sides of the pool, and the team that gets scored on takes control of the ball from center pool at the referees' command.

Variations

1. Depending on the time, the quarters may have to be limited to a shorter time.

Safety

- No running, no glass objects, and no food are permitted in and around the pool area.

Badminton: Individual and Team

Objective

For a player to attempt to land the shuttlecock on the opposing player's side of the court.

Facility and Equipment

- Gymnasium or outdoor court
- Badminton racquets
- Shuttlecocks/birdies
- Net
- Individual and team rosters
- Coin for coin flip

How to Play the Game

1. Games can be played as singles or doubles.
2. Players should have several shuttles to use in a match.
3. A point is earned by forcing the opposing side to miss the shuttlecock with their racquet, resulting in it touching the ground. A point is also awarded to one side if the opposing side commits an error.

Variations

None

Safety

- Be sure that the indoor court is dry.

Baseball: Fast Pitch and/or Slow Pitch

Objective

For each 9-player team to score as many runs as possible. Middle school may want to utilize a 10th player as a rover. A rover usually plays the position between first and second base—like having a shortstop between first and second.

Facility and Equipment

- Baseball diamond
- Bats
- Baseballs
- Bases/pitcher's mound
- Baseball hats (to block the sun)
- Gloves
- Batting helmets
- Catcher's mask, chest protector, catcher's helmet
- Umpire/first base umpire (protective equipment)
- Scorekeeper
- Team rosters
- Coin for coin flip

How to Play the Game

1. Flip a coin to determine which team will hit first.
2. The offense lines up to bat.
3. Defense takes the field.
4. Umpires are positioned as follows: 1 behind the plate, 1 at first base, and 1 at third base.
5. Once the offense makes three outs, the side retires and the defense takes over.
6. There can be 4-, 7-, or 9-inning games, depending on time.

Variations

None

Safety

- Always wear a batting helmet when at bat.
- Practice swings should be taken in the on-deck circle/area.
- *Never* throw the bat.
- Stay alert, be aware of your surroundings, and know where the ball is at all times. You don't want a player to throw the ball your way and you aren't ready to catch it.
- Always know how many outs there are.

Basketball: 5-Player Team Games

Objective

To score more points than your opponent.

Facility and Equipment

- Indoor or outdoor basketball court(s)
- 1 basketball per game
- Pinnies or numbered shirts for each team
- Officiating team including referee, scorekeeper, and timekeeper
- Whistles, scorebook, pencils, and stopwatch and/or scoreboard
- Team rosters: 5-man team consists of 2 forwards, 2 guards, and 1 center
- Coin for coin flip

How to Play the Game

1. One player from each team stands opposite each other at center court. The referee sets up a jump ball/tip-off (throwing the ball up into the air between the 2 players). Whichever team recovers the tip-off becomes the offense.
2. Alternatively, you can flip a coin to determine who will take the ball out first.
3. Key baskets are worth 2 points, outside the key is worth 3 points, and free throws are worth 1 point.
4. The winner is the team who scores the most points.

Variations

None

Safety

- No food or drink are permitted on the courts. If indoors, be sure that the floor is dry.

Basketball: Around the World

Objective

To be the first player to make all the shots from each of the marked areas.

Facility and Equipment

- Basketball court: use half courts in order to have 2 games being played at the same time
- 1 basketball per team
- Cones or masking tape placed around the court (or chalk if outside); these will become the shot spots, 12 in all
- Sign-up sheets

How to Play the Game

1. Begin with 2 or 3 players per group (up to 4 if a team); start at first position.
2. Players may attempt 2 shots from each numbered area.
3. If you miss a shot, the other player(s) can take their turn and you will resume in the spot that you missed. If you choose to take a second shot and make that shot, you keep going; if you miss the second shot, you have to start at the very beginning when it is your turn again.

Variations

1. After going all the way to the top number, begin shooting in reverse order.
2. Switch throwing arm on every other shot.
3. Use the nondominant hand only.

Safety

- Do not allow students to hang on the rim.

Basketball: Slam Dunk Hoops

Objective

To allow students to add a new dimension (the dunk) to their game. It will definitely attract students who always wondered what it would be like to dunk a basketball.

Facility and Equipment

- Gymnasium/basketball court
- Adjustable basketball standards
- Sign-up sheets

How to Play the Game

1. Rim heights
   a. Middle school should be around 7 to 8 feet high (or lower depending on the size of the players).
   b. High school should be around 8 to 9 feet high (or lower depending on the size of the players).
2. Play any game that is played on a regulation basketball court.

Variation

1. Create a slam-dunk tournament.

Safety

- Do not allow participants to hang on the rims.

Basketball: HORSE

Objectives

Try to make various or creative shots that the other participants cannot duplicate. Each missed shot will result in a letter, beginning with the letter H until the word "horse" is spelled out, which would total 5 missed shots.

Facility and Equipment

- Basketball court; use half courts in order to play 2 games at a time
- 1 basketball for each group of 2, 3, or 4 players
- Sign-up sheets

How to Play the Game

1. Participants determine a shooting order.
2. The first player shoots any shot of his or her choice.
3. If the shot is made, the next player must duplicate the same shot.
4. If the second player:
   a. misses the shot, she or he will be given the letter H. The next shooter now attempts the shot of his or her choice.
   b. makes the shot, the next shooter (other than the person who made the original shot) must also duplicate the same shot. If that shot is missed, the next player has a choice, and so on.
5. Any player to acquire the letters to spell "horse" is eliminated.

Variations

1. Use shorter versions of HORSE, such as CAT of DOG.
2. Set up a tournament by using a single elimination, double elimination, or round robin format. Games can be based on a time limit.

Basketball: Hunch

Objective

To be the first to get to a predetermined number of points, usually 18 or 21, and to compete with or against the other 2 players.

Facilities and Equipment

- Basketball court; use half courts in order to play 2 games at the same time
- 1 ball for every 3 players
- Team rosters

How to Play the Game

1. The basic rules of basketball apply.
2. Form groups of 3 people and play a regulation basketball game.
3. The game is played with only 1 key/basket (half court).
4. Two points are awarded for a made basket, and that player then goes to the free-throw line and shoots free throws (worth 1 point) until she or he miss. Play resumes on any missed free throw.
5. The person with possession of the ball must try and score against the other 2 players.
6. All missed shots that hit the rim or backboard must be brought back out to the free-throw line by the defensive player who obtained the rebound.
7. All steals, turnovers, and air ball shots can be immediately taken to the basket for a score.

Variations

1. Any 3-point shot that is made gives that player 2 chances to make the first free-throw shot.
2. Play a game with 4 players. Do not allow any double-teaming of the ball.

Basketball: 3-Point Shooting for Time

Objective

To score as many 3-point shots as possible within the time allotted, usually 1 minute.

Facilities and Equipment

- Basketball court; use half courts in order to have 2 groups competing at the same time
- 1 basketball per group
- Stopwatch
- Sign-up sheets

How to Play the Game

1. Each participant will stand adjacent the key at the 3-point shot line.
2. Have players who are not shooting line up along the key to retrieve the basketball after the shot.
3. Each participant has 1 minute to make as many 3-point shots as she or he can.

Variations

1. Mark 5 areas behind the 3-point line.
2. Each participant tries to make 2 in a row from each of the 5 marked areas.
3. A jump shot can be implemented into the competition.
4. Try to make shots with the nondominant hand.

Basketball: Free-Throw Shooting from Key for Time

Objective

To make as many free throws as possible within the time allotted, usually 1 minute.

Facility and Equipment

- Basketball court; use half courts in order to have 2 groups competing at the same time
- 1 basketball per group
- Stopwatch
- Sign-up sheets

How to Play the Game

1. Have players who are not shooting line up along the key to retrieve the basketball after the shot.
2. Have the shooter stand behind the foul line and make as many baskets as possible within the time allotted.

Variations

1. Add time from 60 to 90 seconds.
2. Have participants shoot with their nondominant hand.

Cross Country (Short and Long Course): Individual and Team

Objective

To be the participant/runner to complete the cross-country course in the shortest time.

Facility and Equipment

- Course (short or long) mapped out using cones
- Stopwatch
- Individual and team rosters

How to Perform the Activity

1. Have student volunteers positioned at various points on the course to guide runners.
2. Race official starts the race and announces results.
3. Place timers at the end of the course to determine the winner.
4. Scorekeeper tallies individual and team scores.
5. Solicit volunteers to set up and clean up the course.

Variations

1. Since you will be creating your own cross-country course, there are no limitations; it can be whatever you want it to be.

Safety

- Be sure that the course is safe and free from debris, rocks, and anything else that can cause a runner to become injured.

Fitness Testing

Objective

To help participants identify physical fitness strengths and abilities and areas of physical fitness that need improvement.

Facility and Equipment

- Gymnasium and track and field areas
- Gymnasium mats
- Softballs
- Timekeepers/stopwatches
- Scorekeepers
- Monitors, tape measure, and cones (softball throw)
- Whistles/chalk to mark off running distances
- Standing and running long jump field areas
- Pull-up bars
- Sit and reach boxes
- Sign-up sheets

Softball Throw for Distance

1. Each participant stands behind a designated line that he or she cannot step on or over when throwing the ball.
2. Each participant throws the ball 3 times.
3. The monitors on the field mark the spot of each throw with a cone and measure the distance of each throw.

40-Yard Dash

1. First put down 2 cones approximately a stride-and-a-half distance between the 2 to form a runway.
2. Next count 20 steps and put down 2 more cones to match the distance of the first 2 cones.
3. Now count an additional 20 steps to equal 40 yards.
4. Use 2- or 3-point stance.
5. As soon as the runner begins to move, start the stopwatch. Use monitors if you choose to time the runners.
6. Stop time as soon as the runner crosses the last cones.
7. Timers relay participant times to scorekeepers.

50-Yard Dash

1. Same as 40-yard dash but count 25 steps between cones.

100-Yard Dash

1. Same as 40-yard dash. Place cones every 25 steps, doing this 4 times.

Mile Run

1. At the middle school level, participants may have to run around the school, a field, or a blacktop a certain number of times to equal the mile run.
2. At the high school level, participants can run around the football field 4 times, which equals a mile.
3. Place timekeepers at the beginning and end of the run.
4. Timekeepers relay participants' times to the scorekeeper.

Standing Broad/Long Jump

1. Stand with feet shoulder-width apart behind the designated line. Do not step on or across the line when jumping.
2. Swing arms back and forth to help propel the body forward in the jump. Bend knees at a 90-degree angle. Take several practice jumps.
3. Jump and land with both feet together.
4. If the area isn't already marked, have monitors mark the distance for each of the 3 tries. The best jump will be the distance recorded. Relay information to the scorekeeper.

Running Long Jump

1. Participant marks his or her starting point behind the line.
2. Lead with the dominant foot and know how many steps it will take before taking the jump. Participants will need to take several practice jumps to know how many steps they will be comfortable with before performing the jump.
3. Use a cone to mark each participant's last stride before the jump.
4. Run down the track and lower your center of gravity on the second to last step.
5. Make your last stride shorter.
6. Plant your take-off foot on the ground.
7. Swing your lead knee and opposite arm upward.
8. Jump for distance, not height.
9. Lean forward to land.
10. Have monitors mark the distance for each of the 3 tries. The best jump will be the distance recorded. Relay information to the scorekeeper.

Sit-Ups (Work in Pairs)

1. Lie on back and bend the knees; place feet about hip-distance apart. Place hands on the back of the head where it connects to the neck.
2. Exhale and contract stomach toward spine as torso is raised by bending hips and waist. Lift up until torso is just inches from thighs.
3. Inhale and return to starting position.
4. This activity is performed for a set time, usually 1 minute. Timekeeper starts and stops the activity.
5. Have participants work in pairs so that one can keep track of the number of sit-ups and count only the *completed* sit-ups.
6. Once the participant has completed the sit-ups, switch partners and the second participant will begin the activity while the first partner counts the sit-ups.
7. Partners relay number of sit-ups to the scorekeepers.

Push-Ups (Work in Pairs)

1. Get down on the ground and set the hands at a distance that is slightly wider than shoulder width apart.
2. Raise up on the hands and set the feet in a comfortable position behind. Participant may want to set his or her feet slightly apart.
3. The body should now be aligned in a straight line.
4. The head should be slightly tilted upward, not looking at the ground.
5. With the body in an upward push-up position, the arms should be straight and supporting the weight.
6. With the arms straight and lower body erect, lower the body until the elbows are at a 90-degree angle.
7. Once the chin touches the floor, immediately push back up into the beginning position. Only the chin touches the floor for the push-up to count, no other part of the body.
8. This activity is performed for a set time, usually 1 minute. Timekeeper starts and stops the activity.

Pull-Ups (Work in Pairs)

1. Grip the pull-up bar with hands and hang. Participants can have their hands facing either away from them (looking at the knuckles) or toward them (looking at the fingers).
2. Participants should pull their body weight up until their chin clears the bar. To count as an actual pull-up, the chin must clear the bar.
3. Lower the arms until they are once again extended (as in the starting position).
4. Repeat exercise.
5. This activity is performed for a set time, usually 1 minute. Timekeeper starts and stops the activity.

Shuttle Run (Work in Pairs)

1. Using the width of a volleyball court, mark the width with cones.
2. Pair up participants.
3. Begin at midcourt, between both lines. On each line is an eraser.
4. When the timekeeper says "Go," run to either line as fast as you can.
5. Pick up the eraser, turn around, run to the other line, and drop the eraser on or behind the line and pick up the second eraser and run as fast as you can to the other line.
6. Repeat this for the time allotted, usually 1 or 2 minutes. Be sure that the participant picks up the erasers and drops them on or behind the line every time or it does not count.

Vertical Reach (Work in Pairs)

1. The vertical jump wall should be marked off in feet and inches.
2. Get into a hip-width stance.
3. Turn to the side, bend your knees, extend your hips, throw your arms back then forward, and jump straight up.
4. You don't want to jump forward.
5. The participant gets 3 chances to jump, and the highest mark is the mark that is recorded.

Sit and Reach (Work in Pairs)
1. Sit and reach testing box will be needed.
2. Have participants remove their shoes and sit on the floor with their legs stretched out in front of them.
3. Place the arms overhead with fingers extended. Participants lean forward and extend their arms and fingers as far as they can.
4. Each participant performs the activity 3 times, and the highest mark is recorded.

Football: 7-Player Flag Football Team

Objective

To score points by moving the football down the field and across the goal line. The team with the most points at the end of the regular time is the winner.

Facility and Equipment

- Football or soccer field
- 1 football for every 2 teams
- Velcro flag belts (each belt with 2 flags)
- Official
- Scorekeeper/scorebook
- Timekeeper/stopwatch
- A coin to flip to start the game
- Team rosters
- Cones/spray paint to mark off the field

How to Play the Game

1. Begin with a kickoff.
2. Offense can throw or run down the field to advance the ball.
3. Once the player with the ball has his or her flag pulled or goes out of bounds, the play is dead.
4. When a team has the ball, it has 4 downs to advance the ball 10 yards or score. Each time it moves the ball 10 yards down the field, it's awarded a new set of 4 downs. If it fails to advance 10 yards, the ball is given to the other team at the point it became dead at the end of the 4th down.
5. Both teams return to the line of scrimmage after each play until they either score or give up the ball and have to punt.
6. The offensive team must have at least 4 players on the line of scrimmage when the ball is snapped.
7. The snap must be one quick and continuous motion, and the snapper can't move his or her feet or lift a hand until after the ball is snapped. Other players have to stay still until the ball is snapped.

Flag Belt

1. Shirts must be tucked in at all times.
2. Players must have the ball before their flag can legally be pulled.
3. Guarding the flag with a hand or the ball is not allowed.

Punting

1. On 4th down, the offensive team can opt to punt. The defense cannot penetrate the line of scrimmage as the punter is protected, but they can try to block the punt only by jumping straight up in the air.
2. All members of the punting team, except the punter, must be on the line of scrimmage, and none of them can move until the ball is kicked.
3. Once a punt crosses the line of scrimmage and touches a player from the receiving team it is a live ball. If the receiver catches the ball, he or she can run with it. If the ball initially touches a member of the kicking team, the ball is dead from where the player touched it.

Fumbles and Interceptions

1. Fumbles and interceptions, depending on penalties, if any, go to the team that recovered or intercepted the ball.

Scoring

1. Touchdown = 6 points
2. 1-point (kick) or 2-point (pass or run) conversion
3. Safety = 2 points

Variations

None

Safety

- Even though there is far less physical contact, players can still trip, fall, or run into each other.

Football: Passing for Distance

Objective

To throw a football as far as possible.

Facilities and Equipment

- Field or blacktop
- Footballs
- Measuring tape
- Cones to mark where the ball lands
- Scorekeeper
- Sign-up sheets

How to Play

1. Each participant gets to throw the ball 3 times for distance.
2. Each participant stands behind a marked line. Upon releasing the ball, she or he can step neither on nor over the line.
3. The farthest distance thrown for each participant will be recorded.

Variations

None

Safety

- Playing surface should be dry.

Football: Passing for Accuracy

Objective

To pass a football through hula-hoops, tires, and garbage cans to moving targets, receivers, and so on.

Facilities and Equipment

- Field or blacktop
- Hula-hoops, tires, and garbage cans
- Footballs in a container with easy access
- Scorekeeper/stopwatch
- Sign-up sheets

How to Play the Game (Work in Pairs)

1. Each participant gets 2 tries to pass the ball for accuracy and time.
2. A bag of balls should be next to the participant so that he or she has easy access to them as this is a timed event.
3. Each participant stands behind a marked line. Upon releasing the ball, he or she can step neither on nor over the line. They will each have 1 minute to throw the ball through a hoop or tire and another minute to throw the ball into a garbage can.
4. The best scores for each participant will be recorded.

Variations

1. Create other types of objects to use in the competition.

Safety

- The playing surface should be dry.

Football: Punting for Distance

Objective

To punt the ball farther than anyone else.

Facilities and Equipment

- Football field/field
- Footballs
- Cones to mark kicks
- Measuring tape
- Scorekeeper
- Sign-up sheets

How to Play the Game

1. Each participant has 3 tries at punting the football.
2. Each participant stands behind a marked line that she or he can step neither on nor over when kicking the ball.
3. Cones will be used to mark the spot of the ball.
4. The farthest kick will be the one that is recorded.

Football: Kicking Field Goals for Distance

Objective

To kick the longest field goal.

Facilities and Equipment

- Football field/field
- Footballs/football tees
- Goal posts
- Scorekeeper
- Sign-up sheets

How to Play the Game

1. Each kick *must* go through the goal posts or it does not count.
2. Each participant begins his or her kick from the 10-yard line (in the middle of the goal posts). If the participant makes the kick from the 10-yard line, he or she moves 5 yards back to the 15-yard line.
3. Each time the kick is made, the ball is moved 5 yards back.
4. Once the participant fails to make the kick, he or she will turn the ball over to the next participant, who will begin at the 10-yard line.
5. The best score will be recorded.

Variations

None

Safety

- The playing surface should be dry.

Frisbee: 7-Player Frisbee Flag Football

Objective

To move the Frisbee down the field and score more goals than the opponent.

Facilities and Equipment

- Football/soccer field
- 1 Frisbee for every 2 teams
- Velcro flag belts (each belt with 2 flags)
- Official
- Scorekeeper/scorebook
- Timekeeper/stopwatch
- A coin to flip to start the game
- Team rosters
- Cones/spray paint to mark off the field

How to Play the Game

1. Set the time for 10-minute quarters or whatever time limit works for your intramural game.
2. Kick off by throwing the Frisbee down the field to the receiving team.
3. Mark the line of scrimmage where the receiving team caught the Frisbee.
4. Advance the Frisbee by throwing it to a teammate. This is equivalent to a forward pass.
5. If the Frisbee is caught, mark the spot of the completion.
6. A score in the end zone is 6 points. Since there isn't any kicking in this game, the quarterback can make a conversion by throwing the Frisbee into the end zone following the touchdown.

Variations

None

Safety

- The playing surface should be dry.

Hockey: Field Hockey Teams (Outdoors)

Objective

To get the ball across the field and into the opponent's goal.

Facilities and Equipment

- Football/soccer field
- Hockey sticks
- Ball
- Shin guards/mouth guards
- Official
- Scorekeeper/scorebook
- Timekeeper/stopwatch
- A coin to flip to start the game
- Team rosters
- Cones/spray paint to mark off the field

How to Play the Game

1. There are 11 players on each team.
2. The game consists of 2 halves.
3. The game begins with the umpire's whistle. The team that wins the coin toss begins the game.
4. The ball is placed in the center of the field. The team on offense hits the ball toward their opponent's goal.
5. The defense must be at least 5 yards away when the hit is taken.
6. Players must pass or dribble the ball with the flat side of the stick.
7. A goal is scored when a player shoots the ball inside of the net within the striking circle. The player who hits the ball into the net must be at least 5 yards away from the goal (the striking circle) in order for the score to count.
8. The team that scores the most goals wins.

Variations

1. Floor hockey/sock hockey, played indoors

Safety

- Do not swing sticks around. When passing or shooting for a goal, be sure that the stick does not rise above the thighs. Always wear protective equipment.

Hockey: Sock Hockey Teams (Indoors)

Objective

To get the puck across the field and into the opponent's goal.

Facilities and Equipment

- Gymnasium
- Hockey sticks
- Plastic pucks
- Shin guards/mouth guards
- Official
- Scorekeeper/scorebook
- Timekeeper/stopwatch
- A coin to flip to start the game
- Team rosters
- Cones to mark off area
- 2 goals (with nets)

How to Play the Game

1. There are 11 players on each team.
2. The game consists of 2 halves.
3. The game begins with the umpire's whistle. The team that wins the coin toss begins the game.
4. The puck is placed in the center of the field. The team on offense hits the puck toward their opponent's goal.
5. The defense must be at least 2 yards away when the hit is taken.
6. Players must pass or dribble the puck with the flat side of the stick.
7. A goal is scored when a player shoots the puck inside of the net within the striking circle. The player who hits the puck into the net must be at least 3 yards away from the goal (the striking circle) in order for the score to count.
8. The team that scores the most goals wins.

Variations

1. Field hockey

Safety

- Do not swing sticks around. When passing or shooting for a goal, be sure that the stick does not rise above the thighs. Always wear protective equipment.

Horseshoes: Individual and Team

Objective

Players toss horseshoes from one stake pit to the opposite stake in an attempt to get a ringer, a horseshoe landing around the stake.

Facilities and Equipment

- Flat grassy surface
- 4 horseshoes
- 2 sand pits 40 feet apart
- 2 stakes positioned in the center of each pit
- Individual and team rosters
- Scorekeeper

How to Play the Game

1. Each player pitches 2 shoes. Opponent follows with same.
2. Players cannot cross the foul line when pitching.
3. When playing teams, half of the team throws from one stake and the other half throws from the other stake.
4. Ringers are 3 points, and shoes closest to the stake are 1 point.
5. The game can be played to 40 points but can be adjusted to fit your time frame.
6. The person/team with the highest number of points wins.

Variations

None

Safety

- Be sure that players are not near the throwing area.

Obstacle Course

Objective

To create, participate, and compete in the building of a challenging obstacle course.

Facilities and Equipment

- Gymnasium or field
- Flat area or hills
- Body of water to jump over
- Hula-hoops to run through
- Short balance beams
- Tables and chairs
- Mats
- Cones
- Balance beam or wooden plank
- Jump ropes
- Stopwatch
- Scorekeeper
- Sign-up sheets
- Your imagination

How To Play

1. Make sure that the course is age appropriate.
2. Consider which obstacles to include.
3. Consider how the obstacles will work in sequence.
4. Be sure that obstacles are far enough apart.
5. Include obstacles that test agility—running in and out of cones, through hula-hoops, or climbing across horizontal ladders.
6. Use low hurdles to jump over, rope jumping for 10 times or so, and a low balance beam (or simply a wooden plank) that participants will have to walk across without touching the floor.
7. Consider incorporating a basketball throw in which the participant has to make 1 basket.
8. Also use strength testing such as a push-up, pull-up, or sit-up.
9. Try to utilize the following in the obstacle course: running, jumping, hopping, and crawling. You will be amazed at how much the students enjoy the competition.
10. Use a stopwatch to time participants. They should be allowed 2 to 3 times to perform the event, each time trying to better their time.

Variations

1. The variations are endless.

Safety

- Be sure the area is free from hazards such as stones and sharp surfaces.

Soccer: 11-Player Teams

Objective

To score as many goals as possible against your opponent.

Facilities and Equipment

- Field
- Soccer balls
- Goals/nets
- Shin guards
- Mouth guard
- Pinnies
- Umpires, whistles
- Scorekeepers, scorebook
- Timekeeper
- Stopwatch
- Team rosters
- Coin for coin toss

How to Play the Game

1. Teams consist of 10 field players and 1 goalie.
2. The field has 4 boundaries: 2 sidelines and 2 goal lines.
3. The winner of the coin toss starts the game with a kick-off.
4. When the ball goes out of bounds, the team that did not kick it out is awarded the ball.
5. A goal kick is awarded when the opposing team kicks the ball over their offensive goal line.
6. A corner kick is awarded when the defending team kicks the ball over their defensive goal line.
7. A goal is scored once the ball fully crosses the goal line of the opposing team.
8. Offside is when the player is either in front of the ball while attacking the opposing team's goal or behind the 2nd player back on the opposing team.
9. Teams cannot be offside in their own half of the field.
10. If a foul is committed during the game, the referee will award the opposing team a free kick.
11. Depending on the severity of the foul, the referee will issue a yellow or red card. A yellow card is a caution; a red card is an ejection.
12. The team who scores the most goals at the end of the game wins.
13. The time factor will vary according to your time frame.

Variations

None

Safety

- Be aware of where the ball is at all times.

Softball: Fast Pitch and/or Slow Pitch

Objective

For each 9-player team to score as many runs as possible. Middle school may want to utilize a 10th player as a rover. A rover usually plays the position between first and second base, like having a shortstop between first and second.

Facility and Equipment

- Softball diamond (dimensions smaller than a baseball diamond)
- Bats
- Softballs
- Bases/pitcher's mound
- Baseball/softball hats (to block the sun)
- Gloves/mitts
- Batting helmets
- Catcher's mask, chest protector, catcher's helmet
- Umpire/first base umpire (safety equipment)
- Scorekeeper
- Team rosters
- Coin for coin flip

How to Play the Game

1. Flip coin to determine which team will hit first.
2. Offense lines up to bat.
3. Defense takes the field.
4. Umpires are placed 1 behind the plate, 1 at first base, and 1 at third base.
5. Once the offense makes 3 outs, the side retires and the defense takes over.
6. Play 4-, 7-, or 9-inning games depending on time.

Variations

None

Safety

1. Always wear a batting helmet when at bat.
2. Practice swings should be taken in the on-deck area.
3. Never throw the bat.
4. Stay alert, be aware of your surroundings, and know where the ball is at all times. You don't want a player to throw the ball your way and you aren't ready to catch it.
5. Always know how many outs there are.

Table Tennis: Individual and Team

Objective

To win the match by being the first participant or team to score 21 points.

Facilities and Equipment

- Gymnasium or flat area
- Paddles
- Table tennis balls
- Table tennis table
- Net
- Individual and team rosters
- Scorekeeper
- Officials
- Coin for coin toss

How to Play the Game

1. The winner of the coin toss serves first.
2. Serve the ball from behind the end line.
3. You can score points only when you or your team is serving.
4. The serve switches sides after every 2 points.
5. When playing singles, the server can serve the ball anywhere on the opponent's side of the table.
6. When playing doubles, the serve is rotated between partners beginning with the person on the right side of the table.
7. The ball must bounce first in the right half of your side of the table and be delivered cross-court to your opponent's side.
8. If the game is tied at the end of 21 points, a team needs to win by 2 points.

Variations

1. Play shorter games—for example, to 10 points.

Safety

- Be sure that the surface around the table is dry.

Tennis: Individual and Team

Objective

To hit the ball so that the opponent is unable to hit a good return.

Facilities and Equipment

- Tennis court
- Tennis racquets
- Tennis balls
- Officials
- Scorekeeper
- Nets
- Coin for coin toss
- Individual and team rosters

How to Play the Game

Singles Game

1. The winner of the coin toss serves first and chooses the side he or she wants to begin serving.
2. The server must serve each point from alternating sides on the base line.
3. The server may move neither over the line nor on the line when serving.
4. Each server has 2 chances to get the ball over the net.
5. If the ball hits the net and goes over the net on the serve, a let or replay is awarded without penalty.
6. If the server fails on the 2nd serve, the point goes to the other player/team.
7. The server must hit the ball within the service area on the opponent's side. It *can* touch the lines but *cannot* go outside of the lines.
8. There are 4 points given in a game and scored as follows: 15, 30, 40, and game; 15 = 1 point, 30 = 2 points, 40 = 3 points.
9. If the game is tied, known as a *deuce*, a player will need 2 consecutive points to win the game.
10. After winning 1 point from deuce, the player is on advantage. He or she will need to win the next consecutive point to win. If not, the game goes back to deuce.
11. To win a set, the player must win 6 games by 2 points or more.
12. If the game ends in a tie, play a tie-breaker; first to reach 7 points wins.

Doubles Game

1. Use the same rules as for the singles game. The time allotted will dictate that you take the simplest route for games.
2. Serves rotate from team to team, but instead of a 2-player rotation, a 4-player rotation comes into play and is used throughout the set. In other words, participants A and B make up Team 1. Participants C and D make up Team 2. Player B serves first on Team 1 and Player C serves first on Team 2.
3. If Team 2 wins the coin toss and serves the first game in the set, this is how the serving of each game would look:
   a. Game 1: Player C serves
   b. Game 2: Player B serves

c. Game 3: Player D serves
d. Game 4: Player A serves
4. In the set or sets that follow, teams can decide which player will serve first for each team and create a new rotation.

Variations

1. You can make your games as long or as short as time permits.

Safety

- Know where the ball is at all times.
- Don't swing racquets around others.

56 / Chapter 7

Track and Field: Modified Decathlon

Objective

To score the highest combined points in both track and field events.

Facilities and Equipment

- Gymnasium and track and field areas
- Shot put
- Shot put circle
- Discus
- Running long jump area
- High jump setup including bar and landing area (landing area must be secure and safe)
- Batons for 4 x 100 medley relay
- Stopwatches
- Scorekeepers
- Monitors, tape measure, and cones
- Whistles, chalk to mark off running distances
- Standing and running long jump field areas
- Sign-up sheets

How to Perform the Activity

40-Yard Dash

1. First put down 2 cones approximately a stride-and-a-half distance between the 2 to form a runway.
2. Next count 20 steps and put down 2 more cones to match the distance of the first 2 cones.
3. Now count an additional 20 steps to equal 40 yards.
4. Use 2- or 3-point stance.
5. As soon as the runner begins to move, start the stopwatch. Use monitors if you choose to time the runners.
6. Stop time as soon as the runner crosses the last cones.
7. Timers relay participant times to scorekeepers.

50-Yard Dash

1. Same as 40-yard dash but count 25 steps between cones.

100-Yard Dash

1. Same as 40-yard dash. Place cones down every 25 steps, doing this 4 times.

Mile Run

1. At the middle school level, participants may have to run around the school, a field, or a blacktop a certain number of times to equal the mile run.
2. At the high school level, participants can run around the football field 4 times, which equals a mile.

3. Timers are positioned at the beginning and end of the run.
4. Timekeepers relay participants' times to the scorekeeper.

Standing Broad/Long Jump

1. Stand with feet shoulder width apart behind the designated line. Do not step on or across the line when jumping.
2. Swing arms back and forth to help propel the body forward in the jump. Bend knees at a 90-degree angle. Take several practice jumps.
3. Jump and land with both feet together.
4. If the area isn't already marked, have monitors mark the distance for each of the 3 tries. The best jump will be the distance recorded. Relay information to scorekeeper.

Running Long Jump

1. Participant marks his or her starting point behind the line.
2. Lead with the dominant foot, and know how many steps it will take before taking the jump. Participants will need to take several practice jumps to know how many steps they will be comfortable with before performing the jump.
3. Use a cone to mark each participant's last stride before the jump.
4. Run down the track and lower your center of gravity on the second to last step.
5. Make your last stride shorter.
6. Plant your take-off foot on the ground.
7. Swing your lead knee and opposite arm upward.
8. Jump for distance, not height.
9. Lean forward to land.
10. Have monitors mark the distance for each of the 3 tries. The best jump will be the distance recorded. Relay information to scorekeeper.

High Jump

1. The runway should be approximately 60 feet long.
2. Before jumping, each participant must have an official or monitor utilize 2 markers along the runway to aid in the timing of the leap.
3. Each participant has 3 attempts at the jump.
4. If the bar falls from its perch, the jump does not count.
5. If the bar moves but does not fall, the jump counts.
6. The participant who jumps the highest wins.
7. In case of a tie, the participant with the fewest attempts wins.

Shot Put

1. The shot put circle should have a diameter of 7 feet.
2. Shot put weights will vary. Use age-appropriate weights.
3. The shot must be placed on the shoulder using only 1 hand.
4. Once the thrower takes his or her stance in the circle to begin a put, the shot should be touching or very close to the chin and neck.
5. Heave the put.
6. Once the throw has been completed, the thrower must stay in the circle and wait for the measurement.

58 / Chapter 7

7. All throws must land within the designated borders.
8. Be sure that the thrower's shoes do not touch the outside of the circle.

Discus Throw

1. Choose age-appropriate discus sizes.
2. Discus throwing circle should be approximately 36 inches.
3. Participants will have 3 tries, and the farthest throw will be recorded.
4. Participants cannot touch the ground beyond the circle.
5. If the participant leaves the circle before the discus hits the ground, it will be considered a foul throw.
6. All discuses must land within the designated borders.

400-Yard Team Relay (4 x 100)

1. Position your runners around the track.
2. Choose your running order.
3. Place your fastest runner first. Be sure not to false start, and pass the baton to the 2nd runner successfully.
4. The 2nd runner should be fast and be able to pass the baton to the 3rd runner without hesitation or allowing for the 3rd runner to drop the baton.
5. The 3rd runner should be quick around the curve of the track. He or she should be able to pass the baton accurately.
6. The 4th runner should be as fast as your 1st runner.
7. As participants are different sizes, adjust your hand-off so that the next runner will have a smooth transition in taking the baton.
8. Be sure that the next runner has the baton in his or her hand before the previous runner lets go of the baton.
9. Keep in your own lane and keep running after you have released the baton to the next runner just to be sure he or she has the baton gripped firmly in hand.

Variations

None

Safety

- Always know your surroundings, and be sure not to stand in the line of play.

Volleyball: 6-Player Teams

Objective

To score 21 points before your opponent.

Facilities and Equipment

- Volleyball court (indoor or outdoor)
- Volleyball
- Volleyball net
- Knee guards
- Elbow guards
- Officials, whistles
- Scorekeeper, scorebook
- Team rosters

How to Play the Game

- Winner of the coin toss begins the game.

The Serve

1. The server must be behind the end line until after contact. If the server steps on or over the line, the ball is awarded to the opposing team.
2. The ball must be served either underhand or overhand.
3. The ball cannot touch the net.

Scoring

1. 1 point is awarded to the serving/offensive team.
2. The team who scores 21 points first wins.
3. A team must win by 2 points.

Rotation

1. Each team will rotate each time they win the serve.
2. Teams will rotate in a clockwise manner.
3. There will be 6 players per side.

The Game

1. A maximum of 3 hits is permitted per side.
2. The ball may be played off the net.
3. A ball that hits the boundary line is fair.
4. A ball that hits outside the boundary line is out.
5. The ball can legally touch any part of the body above and including the waist.
6. If 2 players contact the ball simultaneously, it is considered 1 hit, but the 2 players involved may not hit the ball on the next play.
7. Following the serve, front-line players are the *only* players allowed to switch positions.

Violations

1. Stepping on or over the line to serve.
2. Touching the net with any part of the body while the ball is in play.
3. Serving out of order.

Variations

None

Safety

- Be sure to know where the ball is at all times.
- Be sure to play on a dry surface.

8
Awards

Socialization, competition, and exercise are only a few of the rewards that students receive from participating in intramural sports.

The main goal and objective of any intramural program should be participation and enjoyment. Of course, winning and losing are part of sport, but they should not be a primary focus of the awards.

Some awards should be for recognition of achievement, not solely for winning. If possible, recognition should be available for participation regardless of the participant's win/loss record. Don't forget to include the referees and other officials.

The awards committee would be responsible for creating or purchasing the awards and production of the awards assembly.

With most intramural programs, money is usually in short supply. But each and every school can utilize school resource departments—industrial arts, art, and computers—in creating awards, including trophies, plaques, or certificates.

If your school is fortunate enough to purchase trophies and plaques, you may want to consider a perpetual award. In other words, the names of the winning team/players can be inscribed year after year on the same award. Engraving is far less expensive than purchasing new awards each year.

Another inexpensive way to show off awards is by creating pennants that could be used year after year. For example, if you wanted to honor the championship softball team or the individual's tennis champion, you could create a pennant that would read, "Intramural Softball Champions or Intramural Tennis Champion," with a photo of the team/individual underneath the pennant. You could actually do this with all the winning teams and individuals. This form of recognition, as with trophies and plaques, would require an area within the school for display.

Patches are a great way to recognize all intramural participants. This type of award can be sewn on hats or jackets. You could purchase these for participation, team and individual champs, most valuable player, sportsmanship, most improved, and so on.

If your school can afford it, you may want to invest in T-shirts. These could be given out to all participants regardless of whether they win or lose. This is a great way to promote your school's intramural program.

Whatever you choose, make sure that *everyone* is recognized. This will help to promote the success and participation of future intramural programs.

9

Evaluation and Assessment

The Sports for All intramural sports program values the input of the intramural council and committees, faculty, staff, and participants on how to improve and better meet the needs of the program in which we serve. We would appreciate your input.

The Sports for All intramural council and its committees wants to ensure that everyone involved had a positive experience. In order to help us best plan for next year and make positive changes, we would appreciate you taking a few moments to fill out our survey.

Sports for All Intramural Program Assessment and Evaluation

Communication

1. How well have we kept you informed regarding activities and scheduling?
   Excellent   Good   Fair   Poor

2. Do you feel as though our staff is approachable and that you are able to communicate concerns and ideas?
   Always   Usually   Sometimes   Never

3. Do we meet your needs and/or concerns in a timely manner?
   Always   Usually   Sometimes   Never

4. Do you feel that you received the individual attention needed?
   Always   Usually   Sometimes   Never

5. Is the staff friendly and respectful to you?
   Always   Usually   Sometimes   Never

6. Did the instructors display a concern for your safety?
   Always   Usually   Sometimes   Never

Program Objectives: Please explain your responses

1. Do you feel that the program was beneficial for you?

2. Were you satisfied with the program's goals and objectives, and did we meet them?

3. Were the activities challenging enough for you?

Overall

1. How do you think we can improve the program in the following areas? Use extra paper to respond.
   - The intramural council
   - Activities
   - Rules and regulations

- Participant selection
- Facility scheduling
- Officiating
- Equipment
- Promotions
- Awards

2. Which sports would you like to see more of in the future?

3. Please tell us what you enjoyed the most and what you enjoyed the least about the program.

A copy of this form can be found in the appendix.

10
In Summary

The Sports for All intramural sports program will emphasize three major goals:

1. Movement skills and movement knowledge
2. Self-image, self-esteem, self-realization, social development, and social interaction
3. Opportunity to learn about and implement leadership

Preparing our youth not only to survive but also to be healthy and to function effectively in a society that faces obstacles to health at every turn will require the collaboration of the school, the student, the family, and the community. Working together, we can guide our youth to function more effectively in a world that is undergoing rapid change.

The student who is prepared to assume responsibility for maintaining a healthy lifestyle, both personally and socially, has learned to assess needs, interests, and values; has learned how to set goals; has acquired the knowledge and the skills needed to attain goals; and has developed the attitudes that lead to establishing, pursuing, and revising personal goals.

With the help of the Sports for All intramural sports program, we can provide a comprehensive program to coordinate and facilitate the process of guiding students to accept the challenge to lead healthier lives and to meet other challenges that are inherent in a changing world.

Appendix

Sports for All Program Forms and Templates

The appendix section of this book includes the following forms:

- Individual Sign-Up Sheet
- Team Sign-Up Sheet
- Liability Release Form
- Nondiscrimination Form
- Student Accountability Form
- Student Injury Report Form
- Team and Individual Round Robin Sports Scheduling
- Round Robin Scheduling Template
- Single-Elimination Template
- Double-Elimination Template
- Assessment and Evaluation Template
- Field, Court, Gymnasium, and Pool Diagrams and Dimensions

Individual Sign-Up Sheet

Sport:_____

NAME	HOMEROOM	PHONE	EMAIL
1			
2			
3			
4			
5			
6			
7			
8			
9			
10			
11			
12			
13			
14			
15			
16			
17			
18			
19			
20			

Team Sign-Up Sheet

Sport:_____

Team Name:_____

NAME	HOMEROOM	PHONE	EMAIL
1			
2			
3			
4			
5			
6			
7			
8			
9			
10			
11			
12			
13			
14			
15			
16			
17			
18			
19			
20			

Liability Release Form

Activity: _____   **Date:** _____

I am the parent/legal guardian of the child/children named below. I recognize the possibility that my child/children may be injured during intramural activity. In the event that my child/children be injured and neither I nor any of the emergency names listed below can be contacted, I give my permission to the attending physician to render such treatment as would be normal and agree to pay costs rendered for said treatment.

I hereby release _____
and its employees and assigns for any and all claims for personal injury and/or property damage that may arise from or be in any way connected to the named child/children's participation in this activity. I understand that this release applies to both present and future injuries and it binds myself, my spouse/significant other, and the child/children. I have read this release and understand all of its terms. I sign it voluntarily with full knowledge of its significance.

Signature: _____

Print name: _____

Relationship to child: _____

Please list all children for which this waiver applies:

_____

_____

_____

In case of emergency, please contact:

Name: _____

Phone number: _____

Name: _____

Phone number: _____

Nondiscrimination Form

The Sports for All intramural sports program is committed to providing equal opportunity for all individuals in education. This program shall be free from discrimination, harassment, intimidation, and bullying based on race, color, ancestry, national origin, ethnic group, age, religion, physical or mental disability, gender, or sexual orientation.

The Sports for All intramural council is in compliance with state and federal laws and regulations including Title IX.

Student Accountability Form

Locker Room Behavior

1. All students will be in the locker room by _____
2. After dressing, students will go immediately to their designated areas.
3. The doors to the dressing rooms will be locked during intramurals.

Locker Room Conduct

There will be no . . .

1. Waiting for friends
2. Rough play or fighting
3. Taking of others' possessions
4. Inappropriate language
5. Running or chasing others
6. Lighting matches or lighters
7. Food or drink
8. Destroying school property (vandalism)
9. Untidiness or littering

Miscellaneous

1. Leave all equipment alone until instructor gives the okay.
2. Report all injuries immediately to the instructor.
3. Discipline problems will be dealt with on an individual basis.
4. Stay only in your designated area.
5. No wearing of jewelry.

Student Injury Report Form

Name of Student: _____

Date of Birth: _____ **Grade:** _____

Date of Injury: _____

Time of Injury: _____

Class/Instructor: _____

Location of Injury: _____

Description of Injury:

Trip/Slip/Fall _____ Use of Equipment _____ Sports Injury _____

Collision with Another Student _____ Collision with Object _____ Other _____

Head Injury: Any head injury is treated in accordance with school procedure. Your child has been checked and has shown signs of:

Dizziness _____ Drowsiness _____ Nausea/Sickness _____

Headache _____ Blurred or Loss of Vision _____

Other (Explain) _____

Treatment Administered/By Whom: _____

Was Ambulance Called: Yes _____ No _____

Was Student Brought to Hospital: Yes _____ No _____ If so, which hospital: _____
_____

Parent/Guardian Contacted: Yes _____ No _____

Date and Time of Contact: _____

Copy of Report Given to Parent/Guardian: Yes _____ No _____

Date Report Was Given to Parent/Guardian: _____

NOTE: Parents/Guardians: Please seek medical advice if needed.

Team and Individual Round Robin Sports Scheduling

You may want to refer to this scheduling when playing a round robin tournament. Scheduling an even number of teams will not be a problem, but when scheduling an odd number of teams there will always be one team out. Team X will have a bye for that day/week and will be rotated in accordingly. See example below:

4 Teams

1-2	1-4	1-3
4-3	3-2	2-4

5 Teams

1-2	5-1	4-5	3-4	2-3
5-3	4-2	3-1	2-5	1-4
X-4	X-3	X-2	X-1	X-5

6 Teams

1-2	1-6	1-5	1-4	1-3
6-3	5-2	4-6	3-5	2-4
5-4	4-3	3-2	2-6	6-5

7 Teams

1-2	7-1	6-7	5-6	4-5	3-4	2-3
7-3	6-2	5-1	4-7	3-6	2-5	1-4
6-4	5-3	4-2	3-1	2-7	1-6	7-5
X-5	X-4	X-3	X-2	X-1	X-7	X-6

8 Team

1-2	1-8	1-7	1-6	1-5	1-4	1-3
8-3	7-2	6-8	5-7	4-6	3-5	2-4
7-4	6-3	5-2	4-8	3-7	2-6	8-5
6-5	5-4	4-3	3-2	2-8	8-7	7-6

9 Teams

1-2	9-1	8-9	7-8	6-7	5-6	4-5	3-4	2-3
9-3	8-2	7-1	6-9	5-8	4-7	3-6	2-5	1-4
8-4	7-3	6-2	5-1	4-9	3-8	2-7	1-6	9-5
7-5	6-4	5-3	4-2	3-1	2-9	1-8	9-7	8-6
X-6	X-5	X-4	X-3	X-2	X-1	X-9	X-8	X-7

10 Teams

1-2	1-10	1-9	1-8	1-7	1-6	1-5	1-4	1-3
10-3	9-2	8-10	7-9	6-8	5-7	4-6	3-5	2-4
9-4	8-3	7-2	6-10	5-9	4-8	3-7	2-6	10-5
8-5	7-4	6-3	5-2	4-10	3-9	2-8	10-7	9-6
7-6	6-5	5-4	4-3	3-2	2-10	10-9	9-8	8-7

3 Team Round Robin

Team	Wins	Losses
1.		
2.		
3.		

Round 1	Round 2	Round 3
1 vs 2	2 vs 3	3 vs 1
3 Bye	1 Bye	2 Bye

4 Team Round Robin

Team	Wins	Losses
1.		
2.		
3.		
4.		

Round 1	Round 2	Round 3
2 vs 1	4 vs 2	4 vs 1
3 vs 4	1 vs 3	2 vs 3

5 Team Round Robin

Team	Wins	Losses
1.		
2.		
3.		
4.		
5.		

Round 1	Round 2	Round 3	Round 4	Round 5
1 vs 4	3 vs 1	5 vs 3	2 vs 5	4 vs 2
2 vs 3	4 vs 5	1 vs 2	3 vs 4	5 vs 1
5-Bye	2-Bye	4-Bye	1-Bye	3-Bye

6 Team Round Robin

Team	Wins	Losses
1.		
2.		
3.		
4.		
5.		
6.		

Round 1	Round 2	Round 3	Round 4	Round 5
2 vs 1	3 vs 4	6 vs 4	4 vs 1	5 vs 6
3 vs 6	6 vs 1	2 vs 3	5 vs 3	1 vs 3
4 vs 5	2 vs 5	1 vs 5	6 vs 2	4 vs 2

7 Team Round Robin

Team	Wins	Losses
1.		
2.		
3.		
4.		
5.		
6.		
7.		

Round 1	Round 2	Round 3	Round 4	Round 5	Round 6	Round 7
1 vs 6	4 vs 2	2 vs 7	5 vs 3	3 vs 1	6 vs 4	7 vs 5
2 vs 5	5 vs 1	3 vs 6	6 vs 2	4 vs 7	7 vs 3	1 vs 4
3 vs 4	6 vs 7	4 vs 5	7 vs 1	5 vs 6	1 vs 2	2 vs 3
7-Bye	3-Bye	1-Bye	4-Bye	2-Bye	5-Bye	6-Bye

8 Team Round Robin

Team	Wins	Losses
1.		
2.		
3.		
4.		
5.		
6.		
7.		
8.		

Round 1	Round 2	Round 3	Round 4	Round 5	Round 6	Round 7
2 vs 1	3 vs 4	6 vs 2	7 vs 5	1 vs 3	4 vs 5	7 vs 3
3 vs 8	1 vs 7	7 vs 8	8 vs 4	4 vs 2	8 vs 1	8 vs 2
4 vs 7	8 vs 6	4 vs 1	2 vs 3	5 vs 8	2 vs 7	1 vs 5
5 vs 6	2 vs 5	5 vs 3	6 vs 1	6 vs 7	3 vs 6	6 vs 4

9 Team Round Robin

Team	Wins	Losses
1.		
2.		
3.		
4.		
5.		
6.		
7.		
8.		
9.		

Round 1	Round 2	Round 3	Round 4	Round 5	Round 6	Round 7	Round 8	Round 9
1 vs 8	5 vs 3	2 vs 9	6 vs 4	3 vs 1	7 vs 5	4 vs 2	8 vs 6	9 vs 7
2 vs 7	6 vs 2	3 vs 8	7 vs 3	4 vs 9	8 vs 4	5 vs 1	9 vs 5	1 vs 6
3 vs 6	7 vs 1	4 vs 7	8 vs 2	5 vs 8	9 vs 3	6 vs 9	1 vs 4	2 vs 5
4 vs 5	8 vs 9	5 vs 6	9 vs 1	6 vs 7	1 vs 2	7 vs 8	2 vs 3	3 vs 4
9-Bye	4-Bye	1-Bye	5-Bye	2-Bye	6-Bye	3-Bye	7-Bye	8-Bye

10 Team Round Robin

Team	Wins	Losses
1.		
2.		
3.		
4.		
5.		
6.		
7.		
8.		
9.		
10.		

Round 1	Round 2	Round 3	Round 4	Round 5	Round 6	Round 7	Round 8	Round 9
2 vs 1	2 vs 3	6 vs 9	10 vs 6	5 vs 3	1 vs 9	5 vs 1	5 vs 6	9 vs 3
3 vs 10	1 vs 7	7 vs 8	2 vs 5	6 vs 2	10 vs 8	6 vs 4	1 vs 10	10 vs 2
4 vs 9	8 vs 6	3 vs 1	3 vs 4	7 vs 10	2 vs 7	7 vs 3	2 vs 9	6 vs 1
5 vs 8	9 vs 5	4 vs 2	1 vs 8	8 vs 9	3 vs 6	8 vs 2	3 vs 8	7 vs 5
6 vs 7	10 vs 4	5 vs 10	9 vs 7	4 vs 1	4 vs 5	9 vs 10	4 vs 7	8 vs 4

Appendix / 85

Single-Elimination Template

3 Team Single Elimination

Winner

4 Team Single Elimination

Winner

5 Team Single Elimination

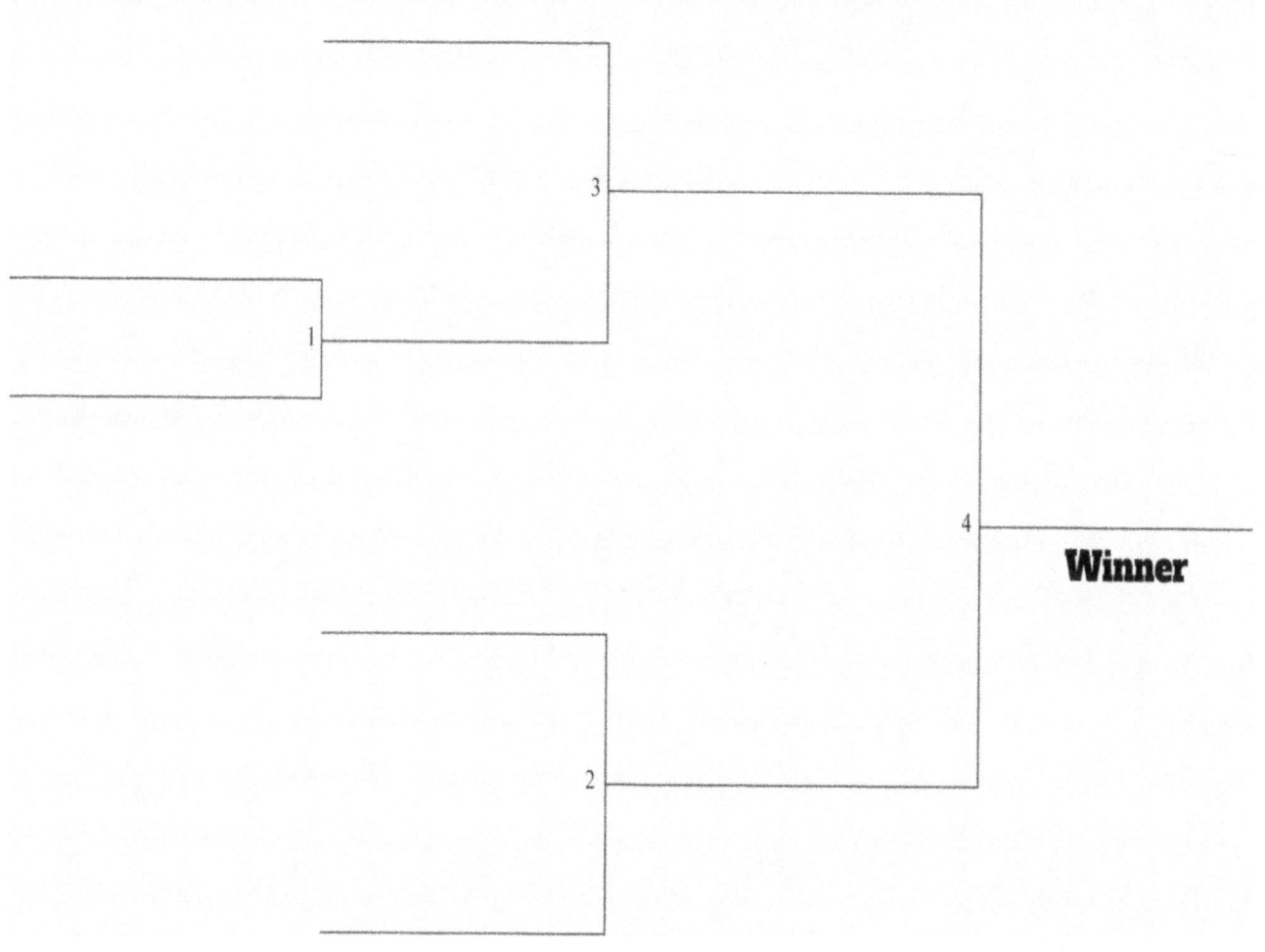

6 Team Single Elimination

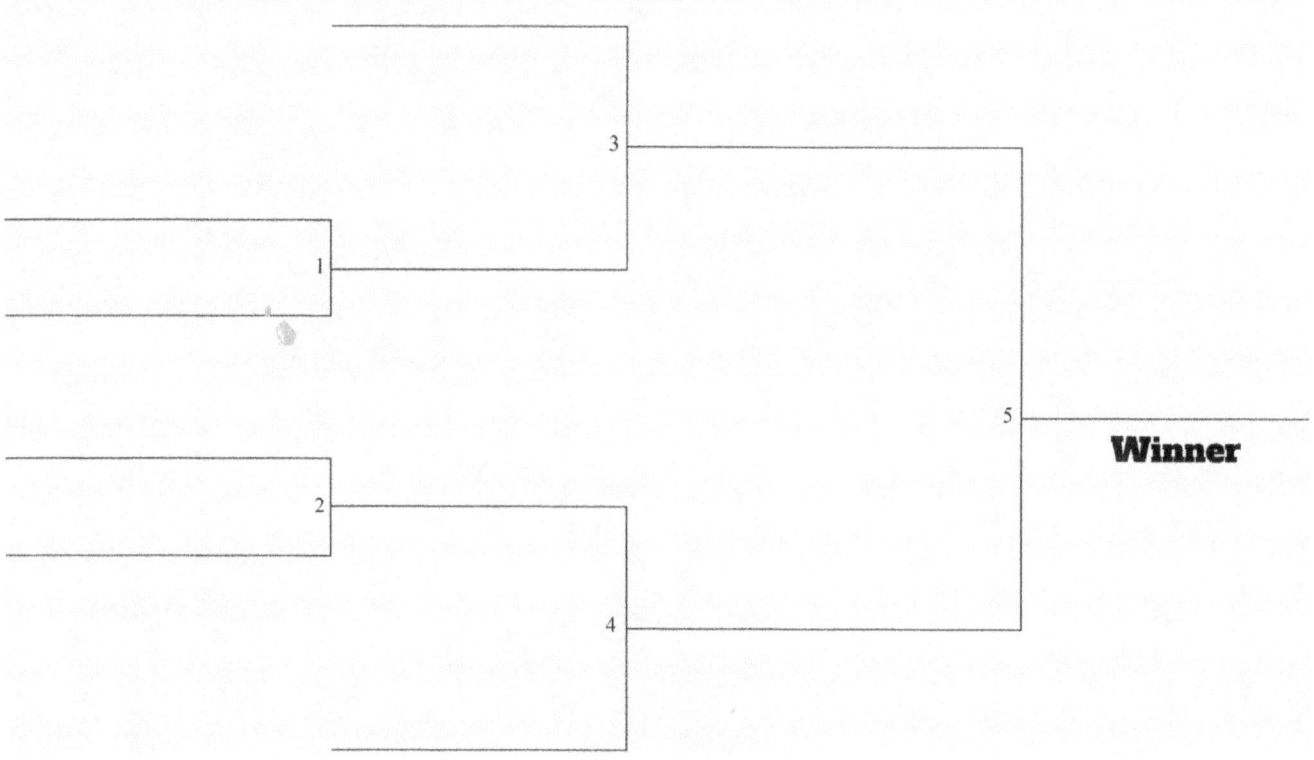

7 Team Single Elimination

8 Team Single Elimination

Winner

9 Team Single Elimination

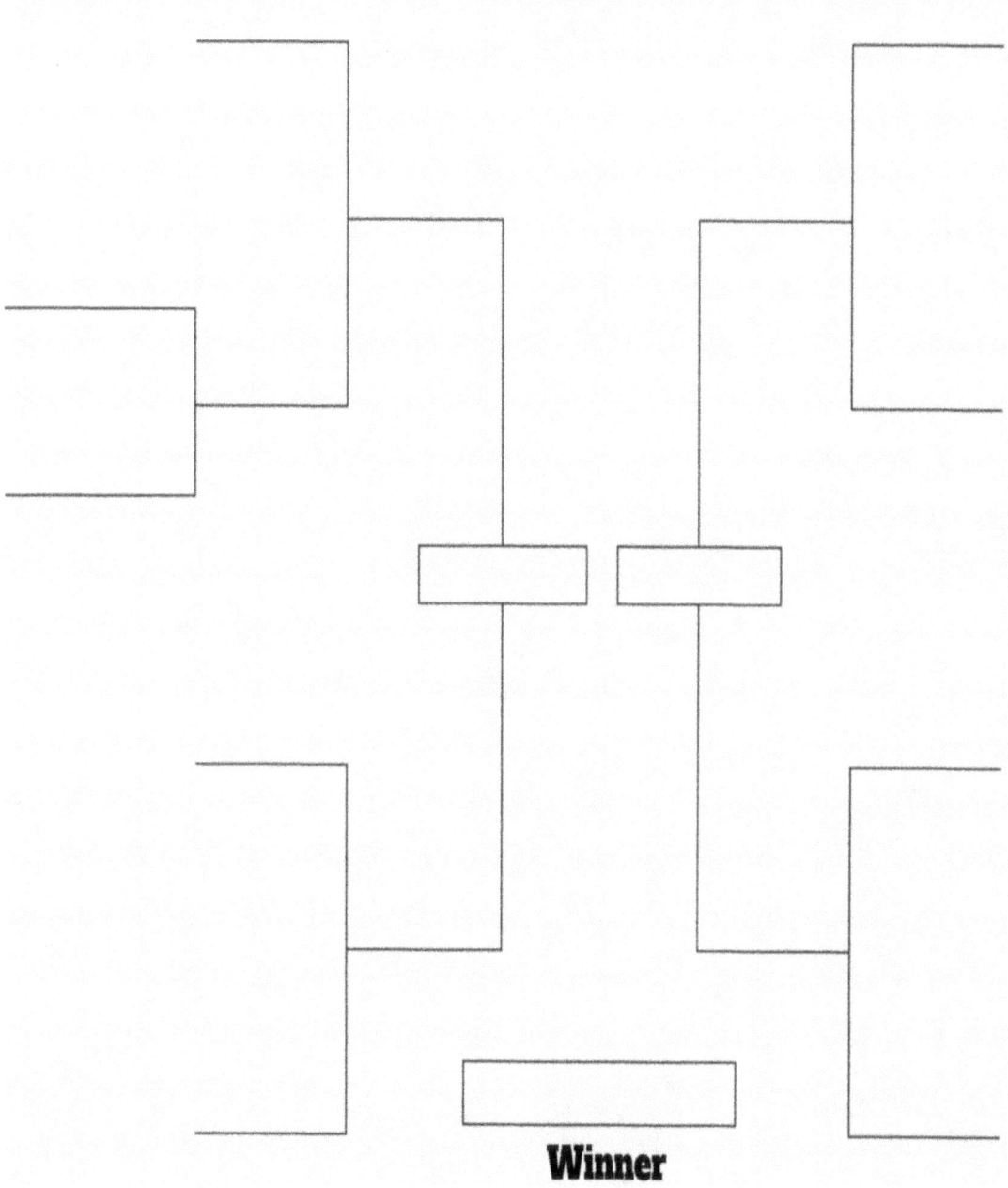

Winner

10 Team Single Elimination

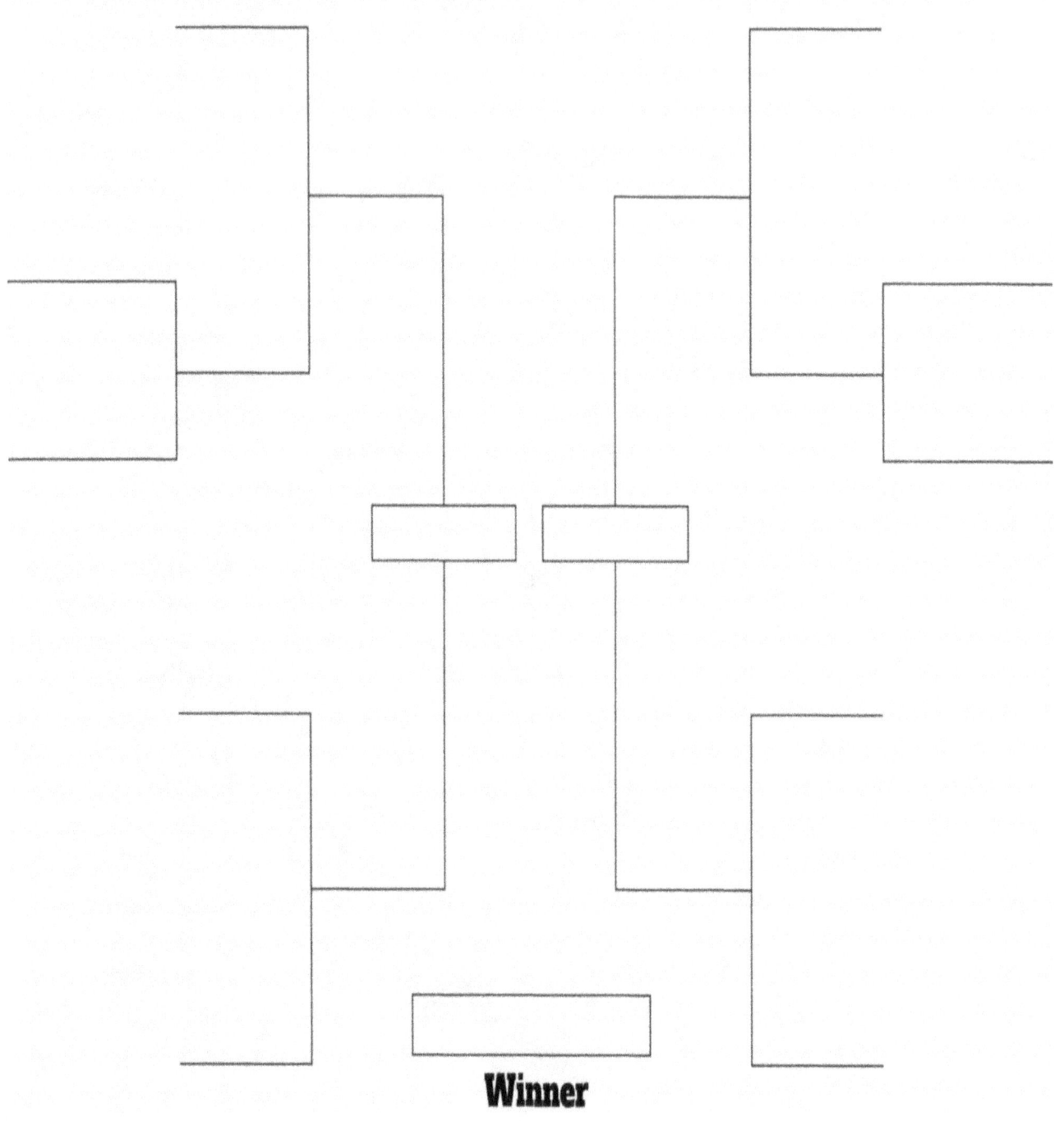

Winner

Appendix / 93

Double-Elimination Template

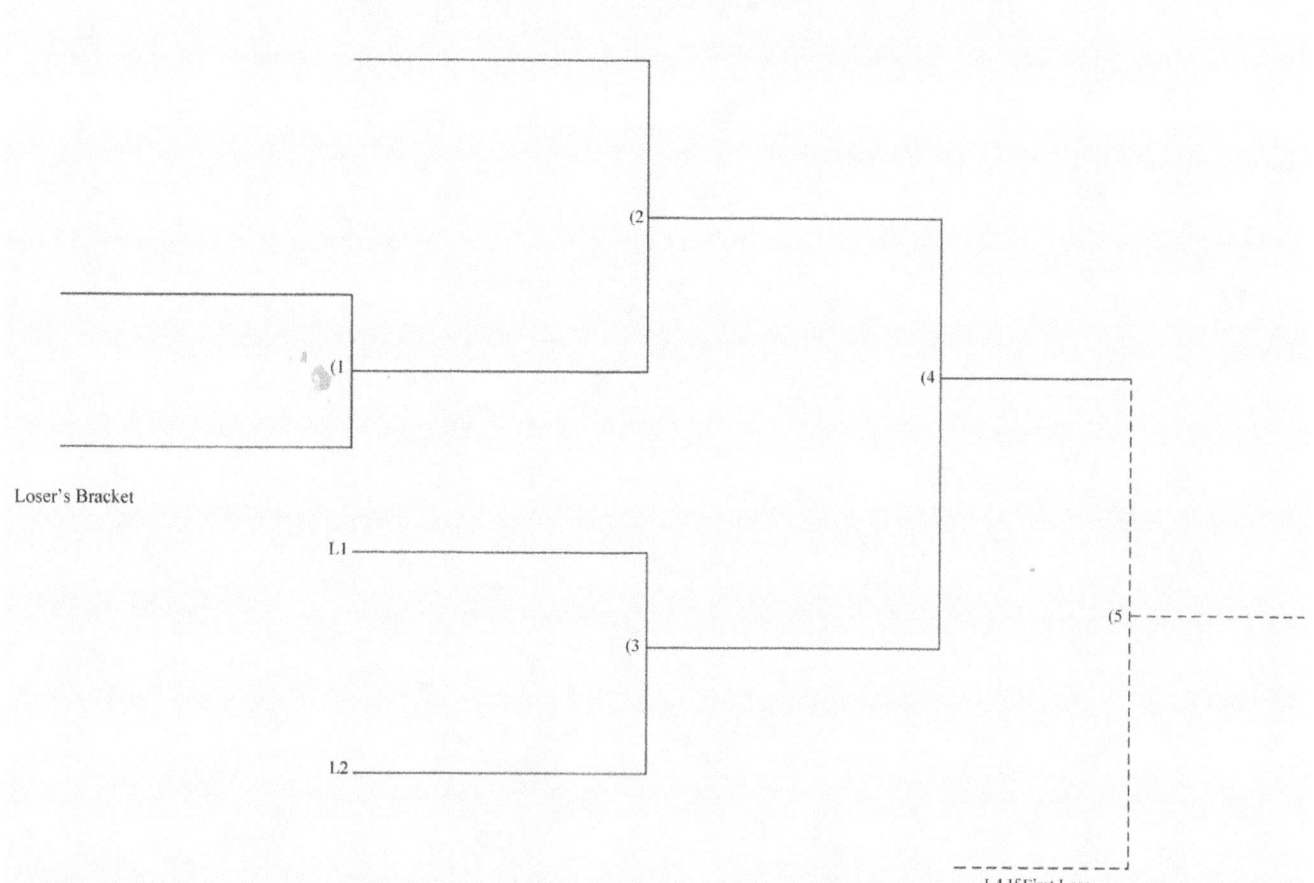

4 Team Double Elimination

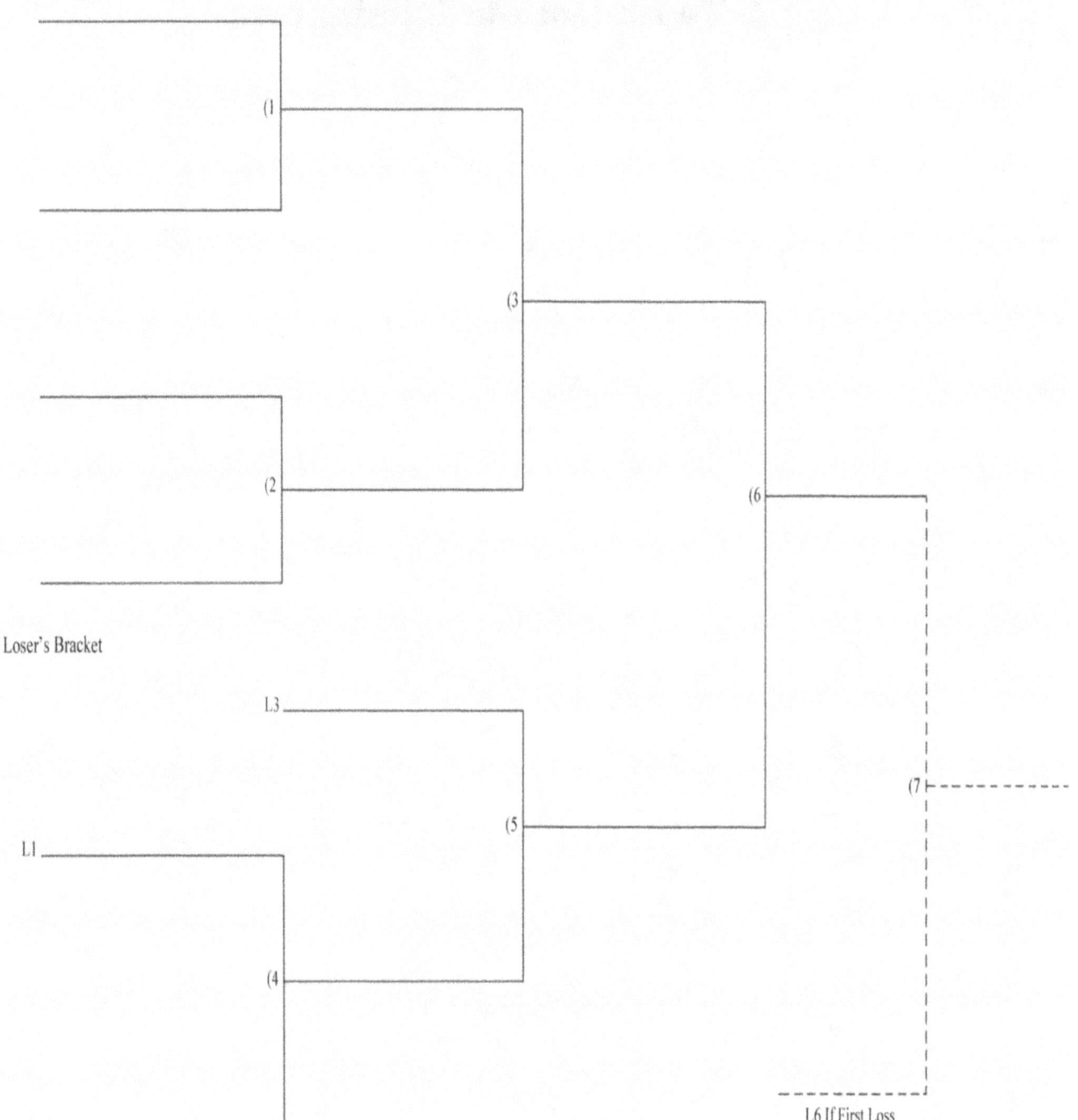

5 Team Double Elimination

Winner's Bracket

Loser's Bracket

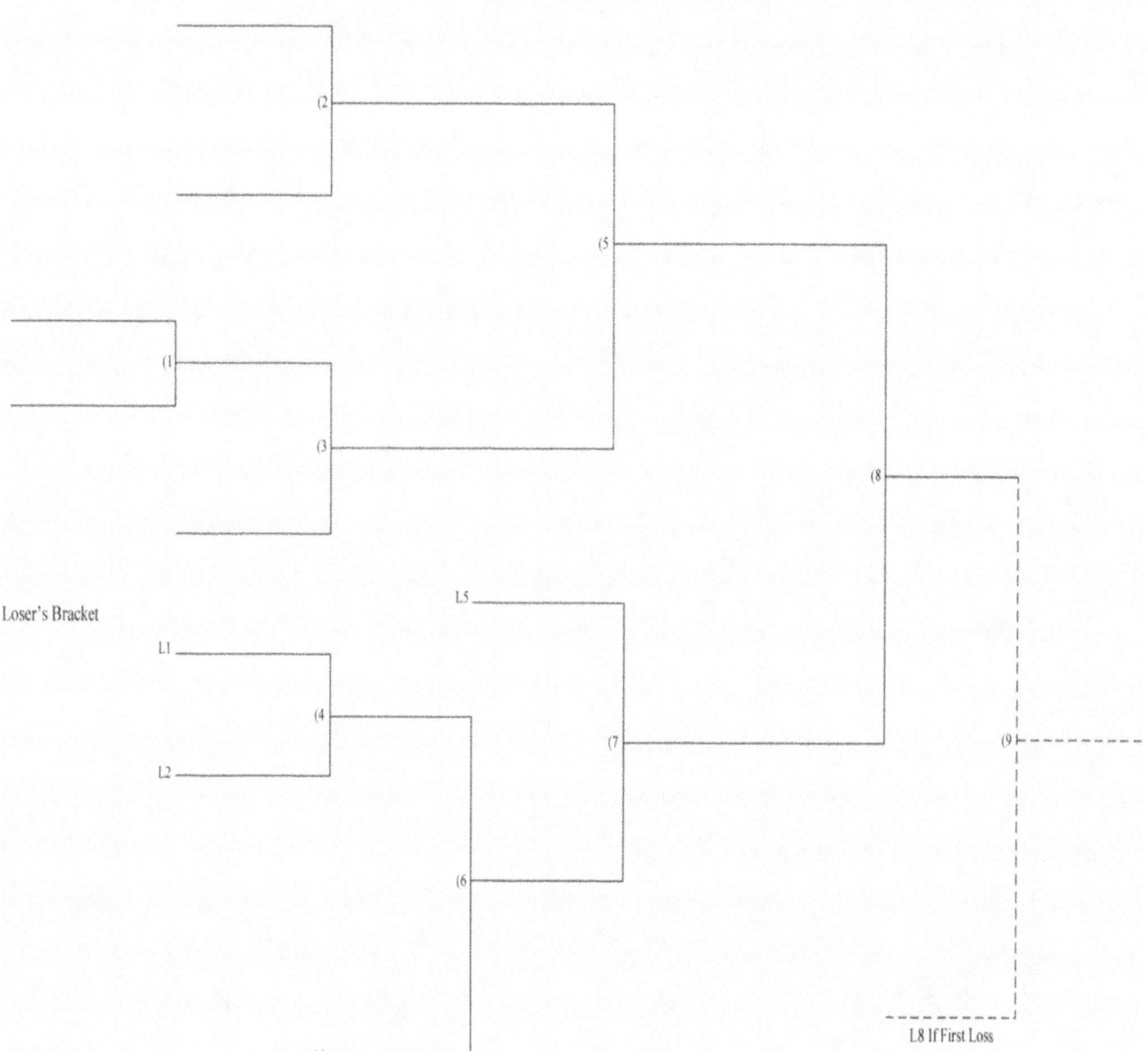

L8 If First Loss

Winner's Bracket

6 Team Double Elimination

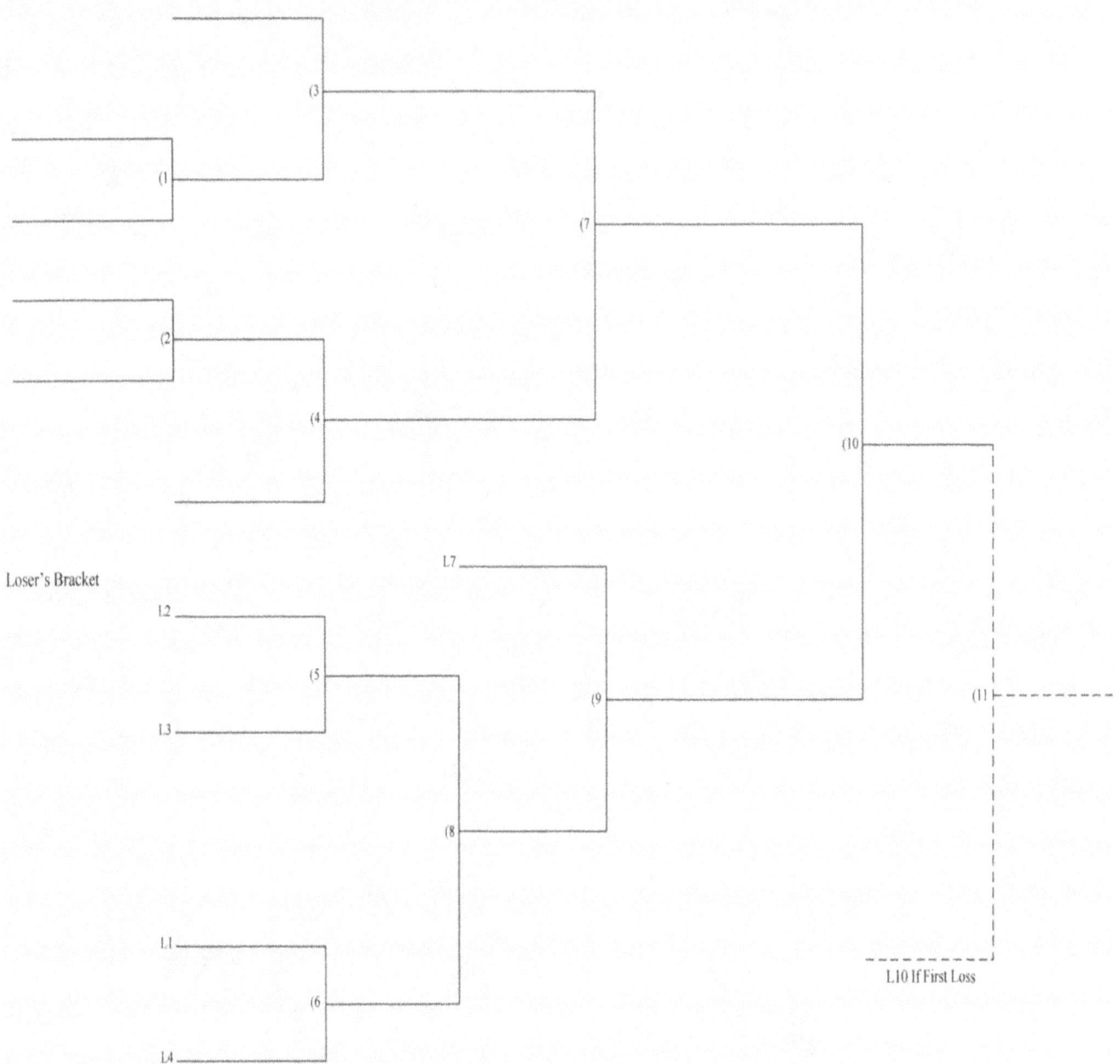

Loser's Bracket

L10 If First Loss

7 Team Double Tournament

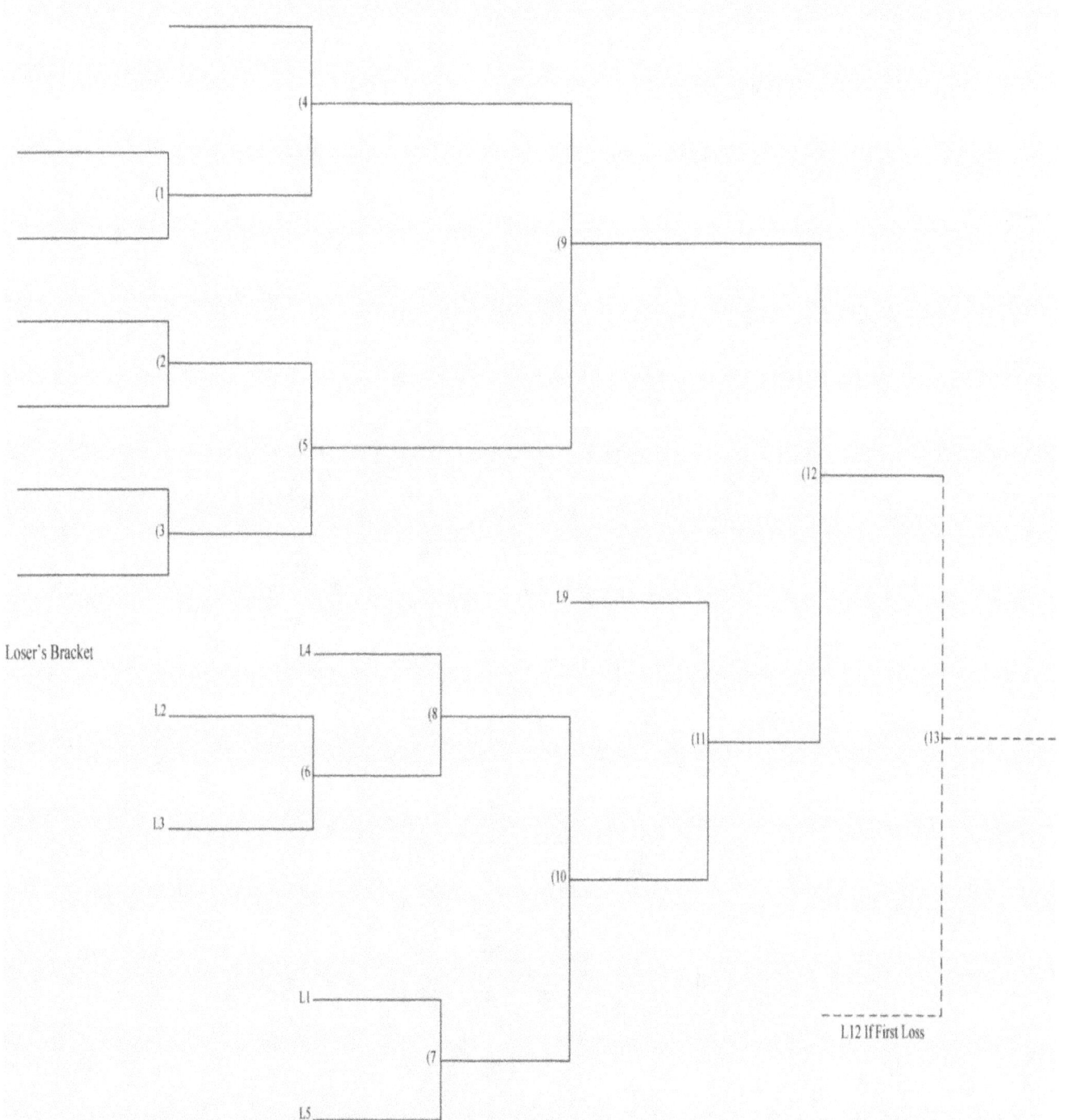

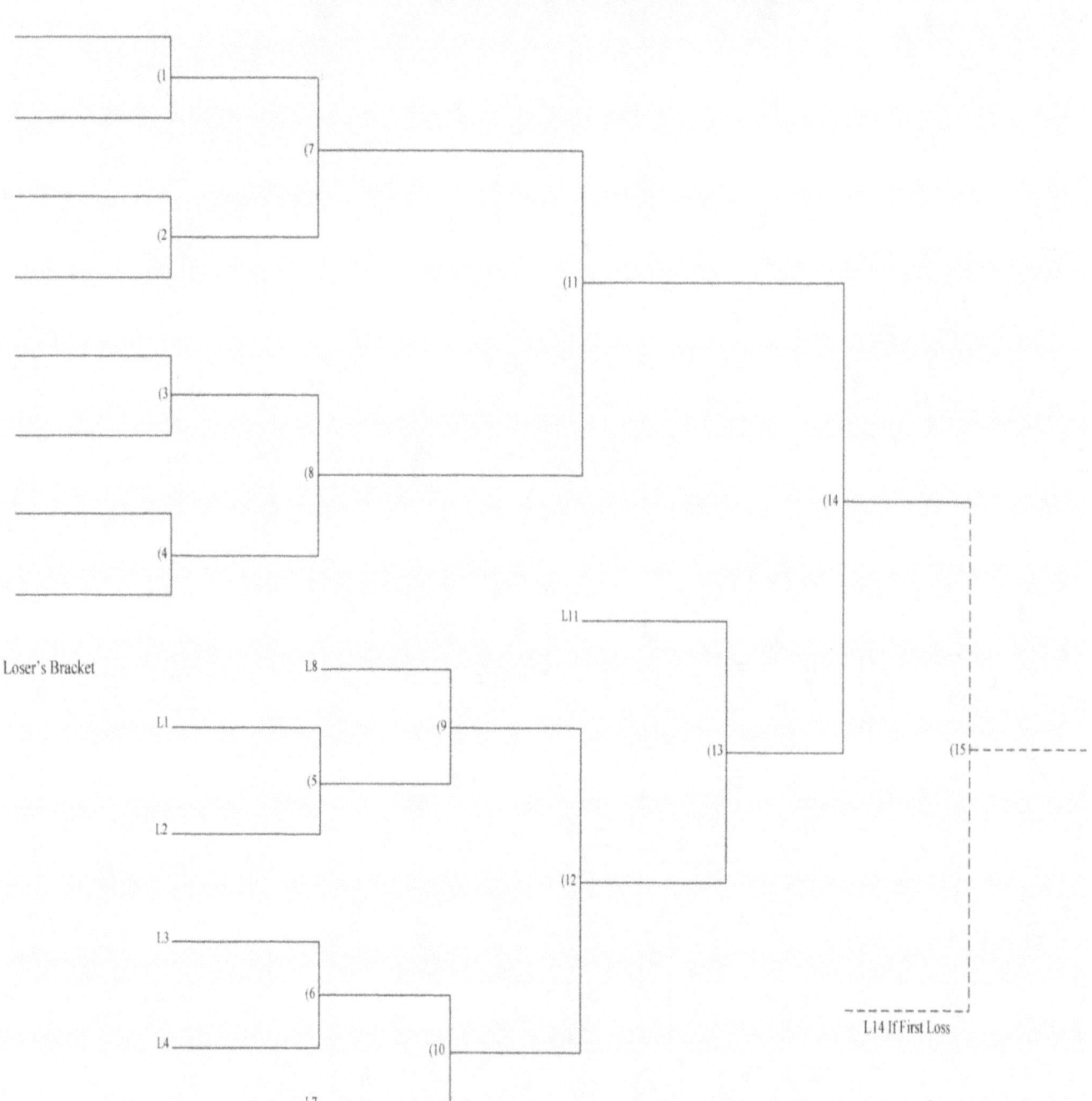

9 Team Double Elimination

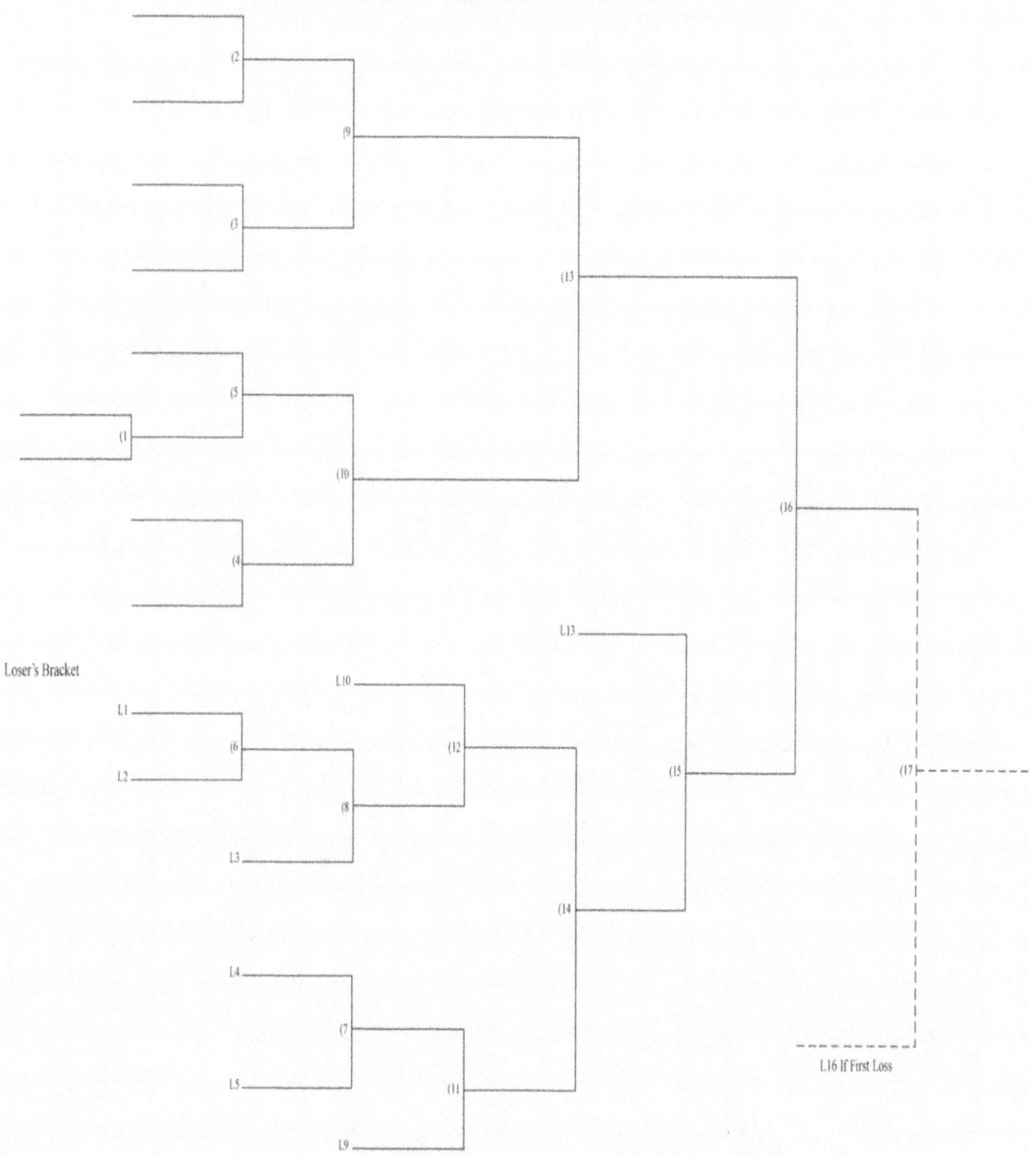

10 Team Double Elimination

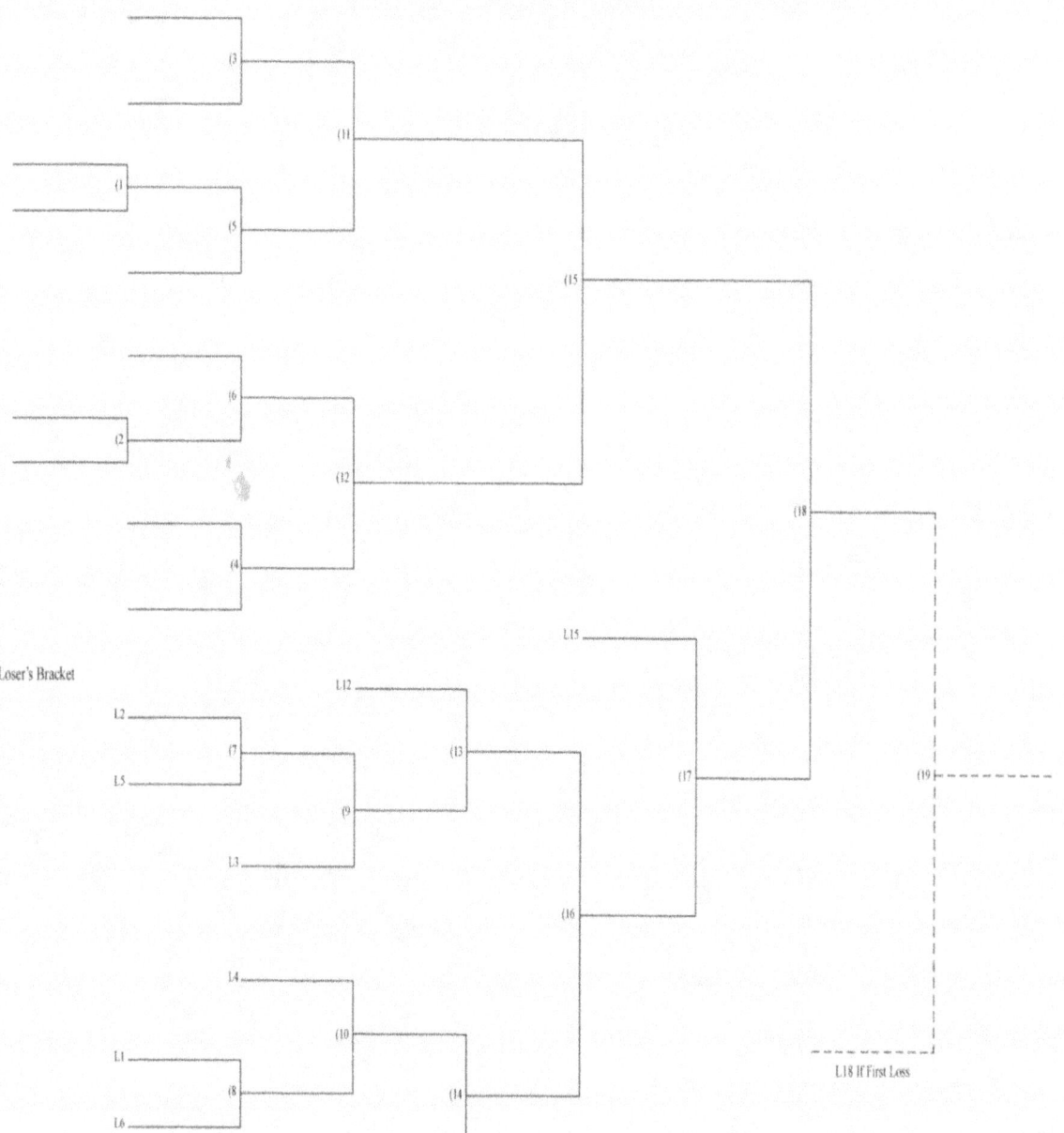

Assessment and Evaluation Template

The Sports for All intramural sports program values its intramural council and committees', faculty staff's, and participants' input on how to improve and better meet the needs of the program in which we serve. We would appreciate your input.

The intramural council and its committees want to ensure that everyone involved had a positive experience. In order to help us best plan for next year and make positive changes, we would appreciate you taking a few moments to fill out our survey.

Communication

1. How well have we kept you informed regarding activities and scheduling?
   Excellent   Good   Fair   Poor

2. Do you feel as though our staff is approachable and that you are able to communicate concerns and ideas?
   Always   Usually   Sometimes   Never

3. Do we meet your needs and/or concerns in a timely manner?
   Always   Usually   Sometimes   Never

4. Do you feel that you received the individual attention needed?
   Always   Usually   Sometimes   Never

5. Is the staff friendly and respectful to you?
   Always   Usually   Sometimes   Never

6. Did the instructors display a concern for your safety?
   Always   Usually   Sometimes   Never

Program Objectives: Please explain your responses
1. Do you feel that the program was beneficial for you?

2. Were you satisfied with the program's goals and objectives, and did we meet them?

3. Were the activities challenging enough for you?

Overall
1. How do you think we can improve the program in the following areas? Use extra paper to respond.
   a. The intramural council
   b. Activities
   c. Rules and regulations
   d. Participant selection
   e. Facility scheduling
   f. Officiating
   g. Equipment
   h. Promotions
   i. Awards

2. Which sports would you like to see more of in the future?

Please tell us what you enjoyed the most and what you enjoyed the least about the program.

Field, Court, Gymnasium, and Pool Diagrams and Dimensions

Badminton Court Dimensions

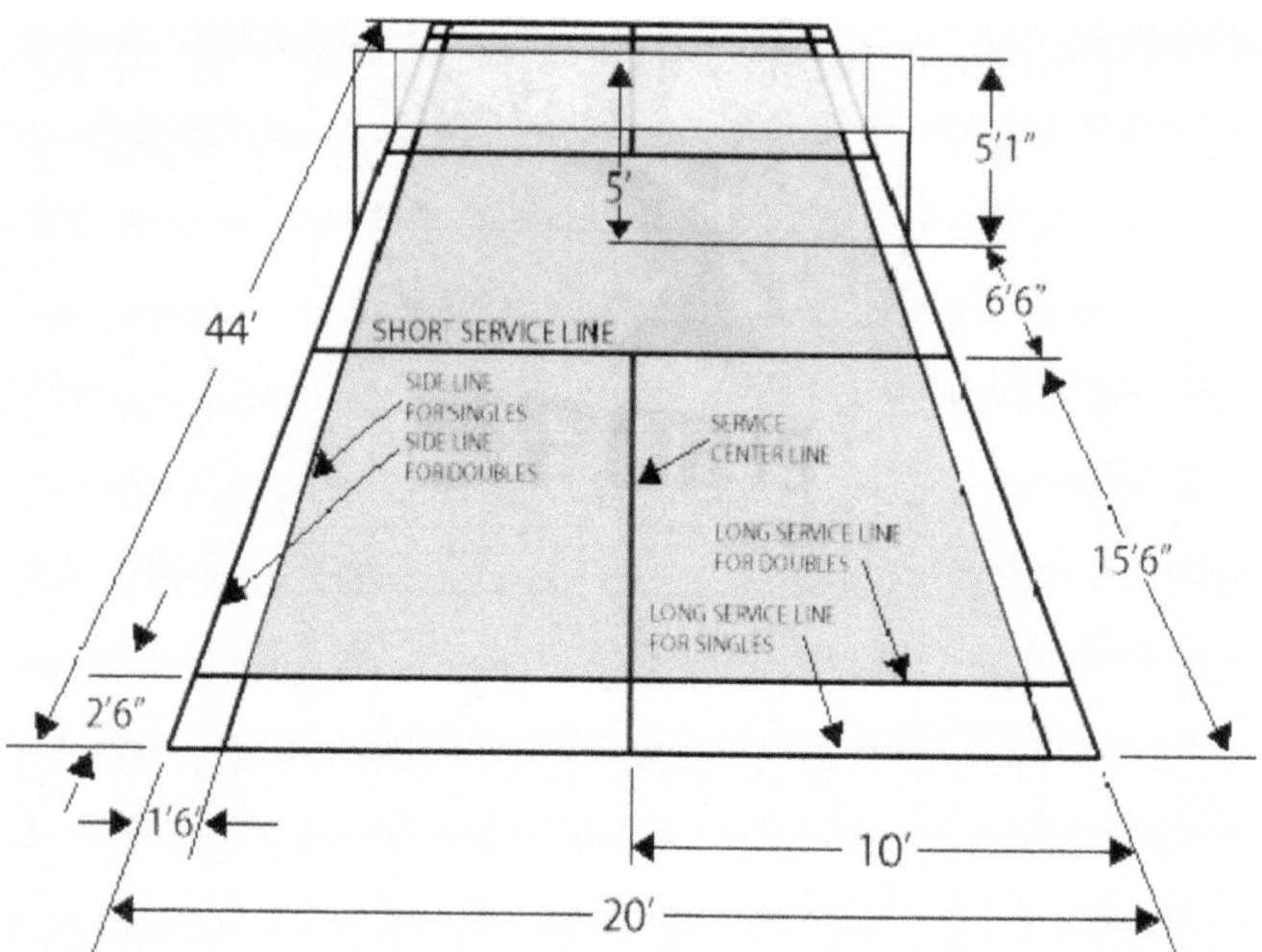

Baseball Field Dimensions

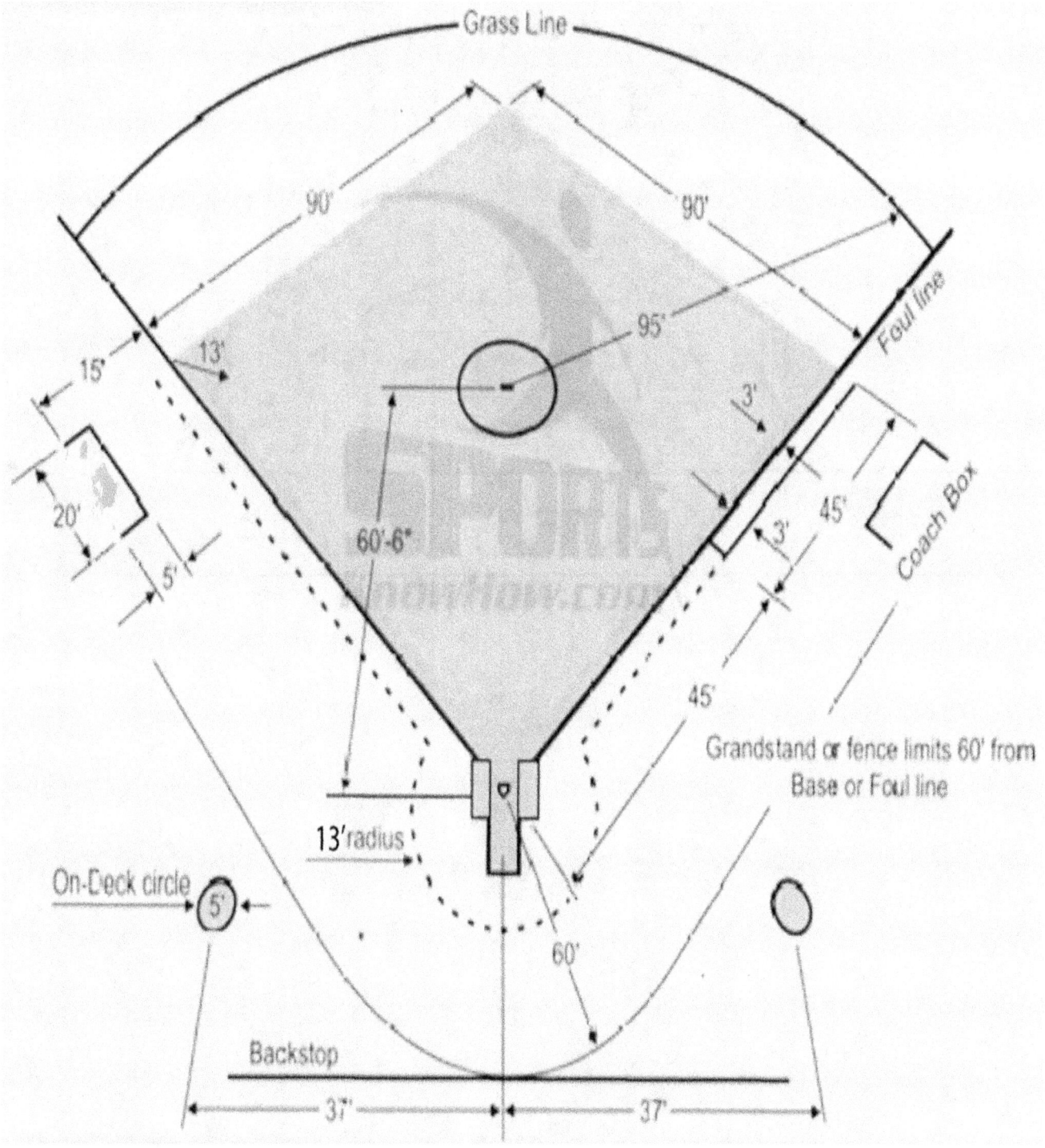

Basketball Court Dimensions

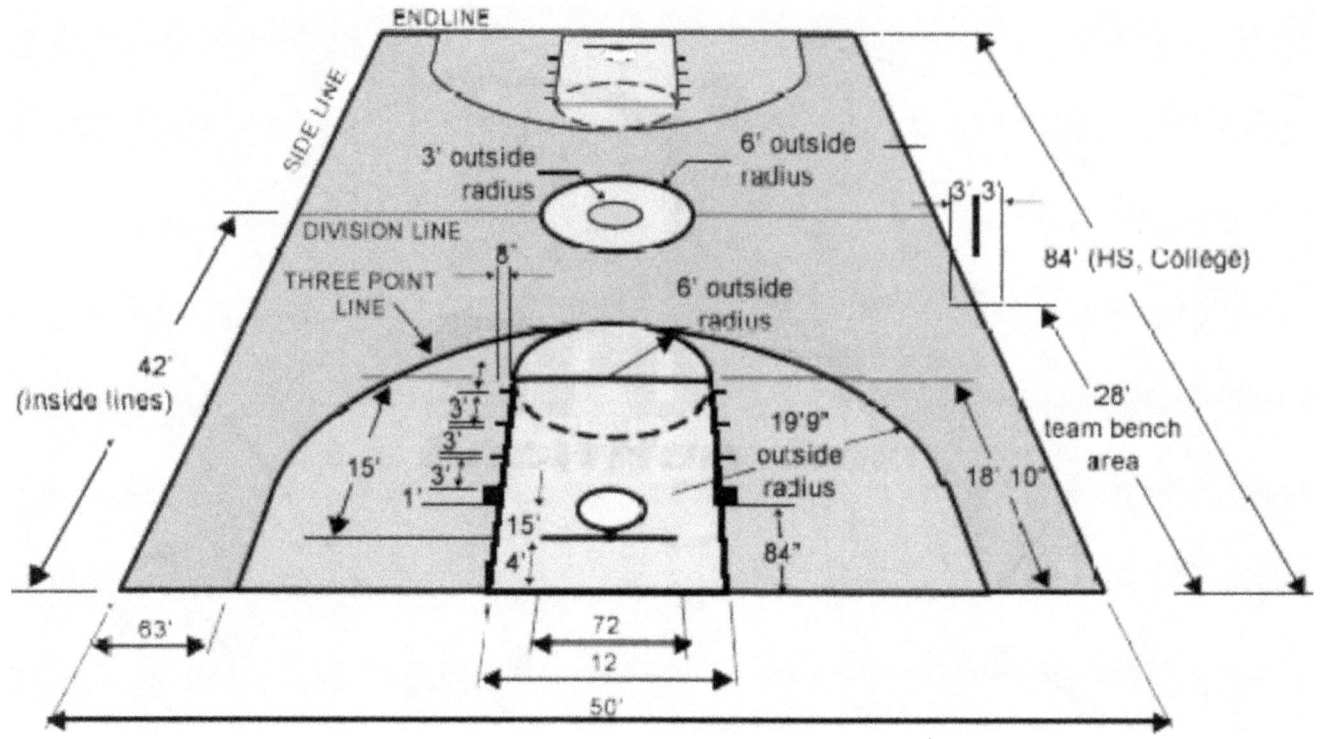

Flag Football Field Dimensions

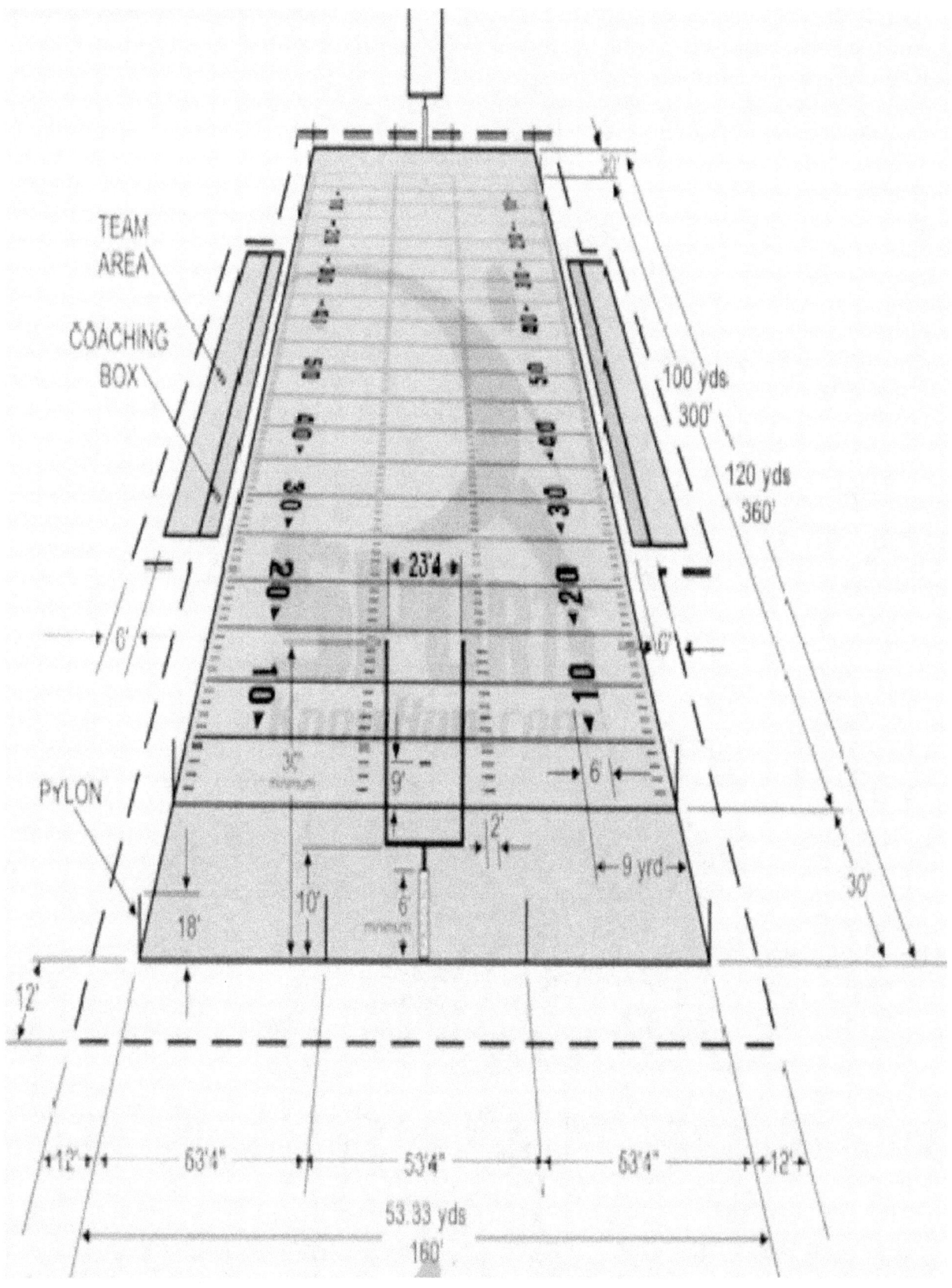

Field Hockey Field Dimensions

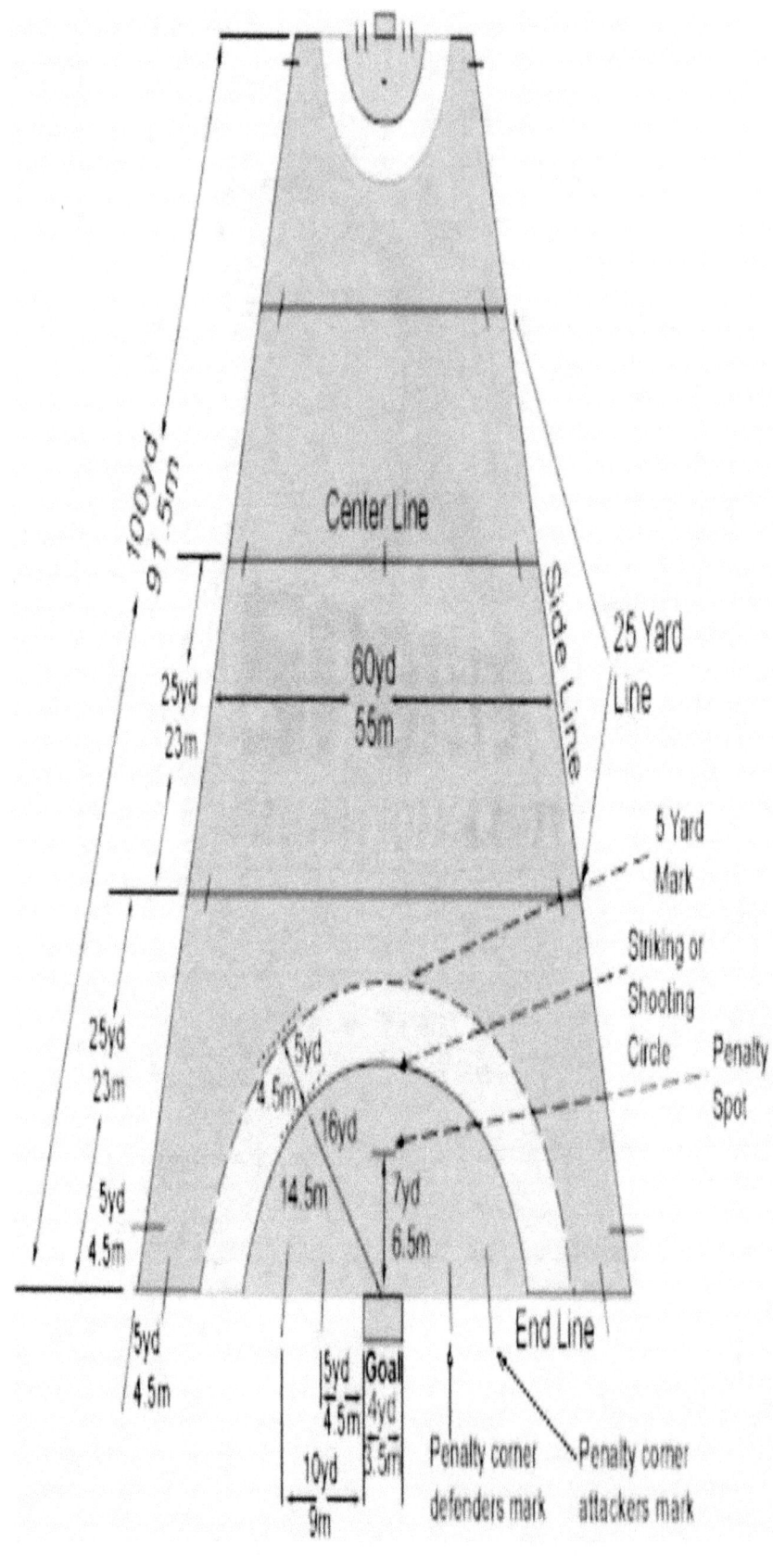

Horseshoe Pit Dimensions

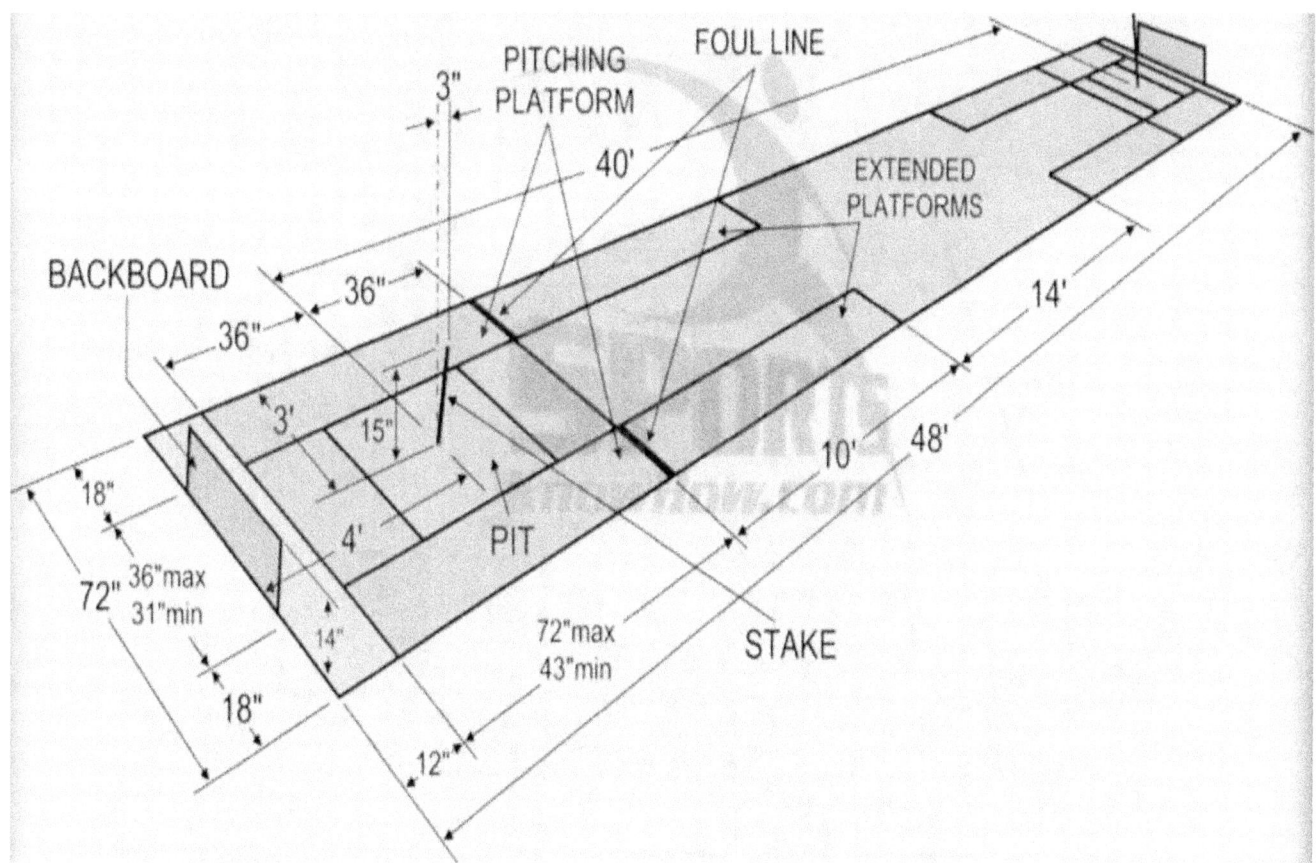

Soccer Field Dimensions

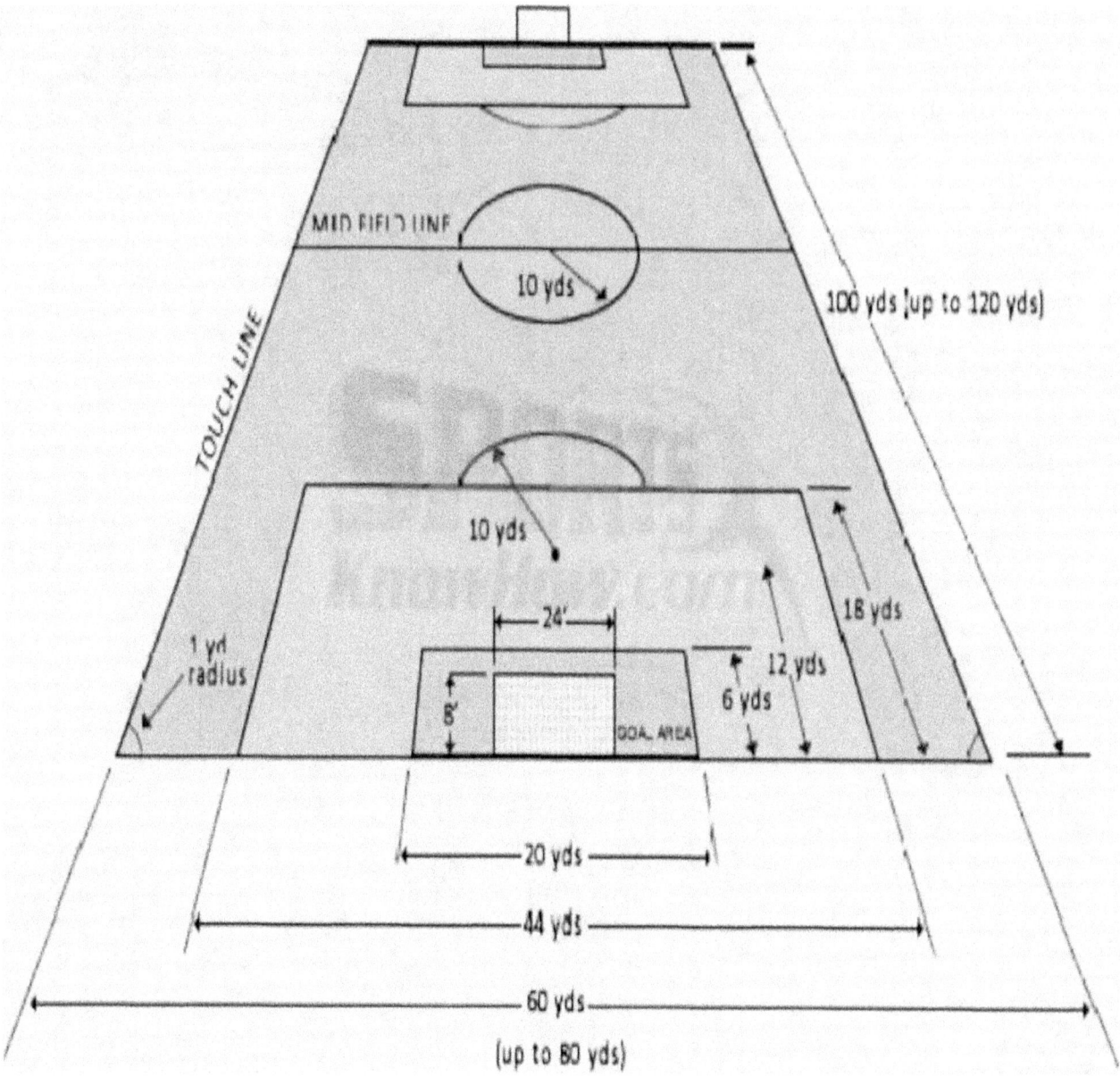

Appendix / 111

Softball Field Dimensions: Fast Pitch

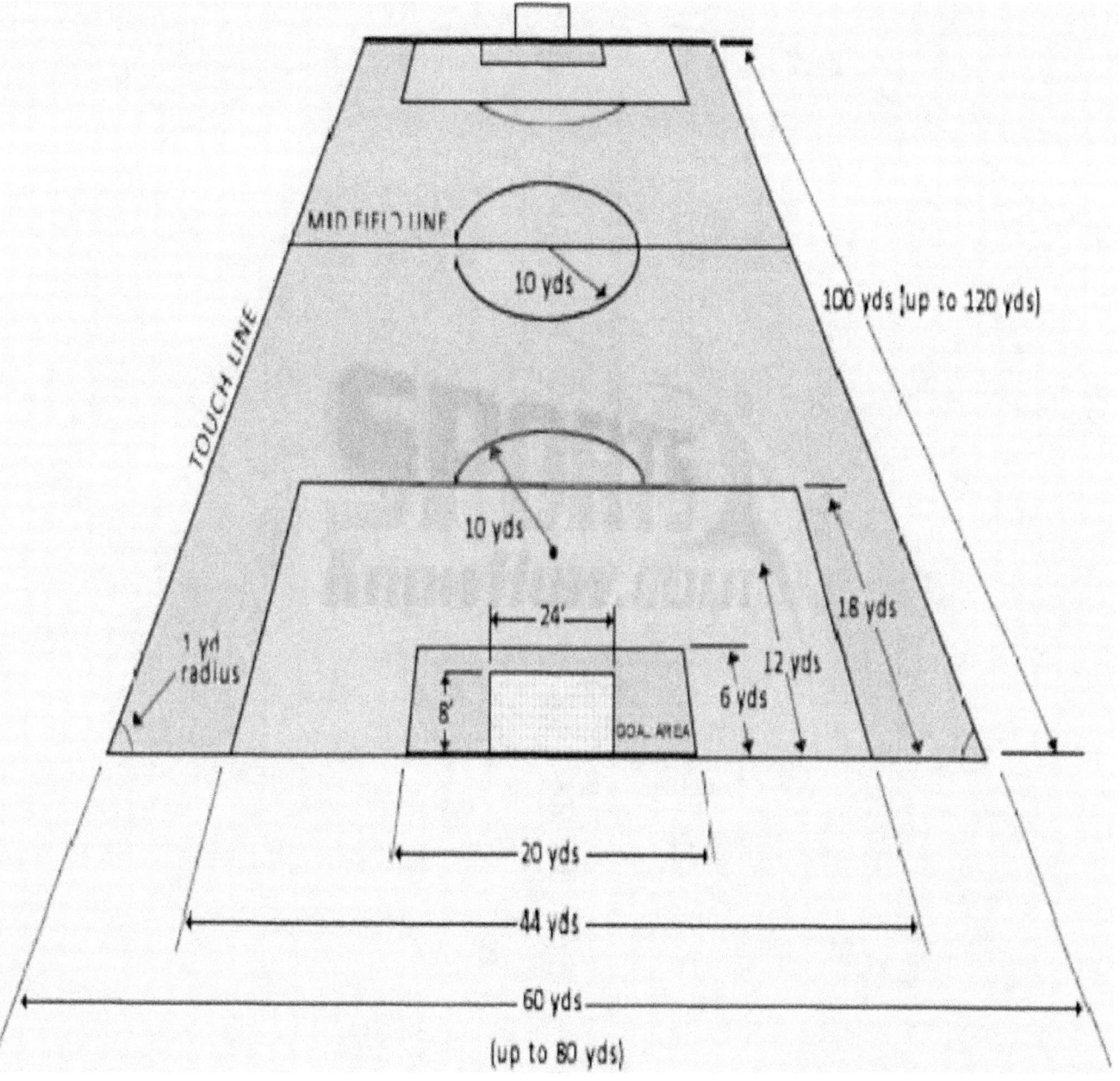

Softball Field Dimensions: Slow Pitch

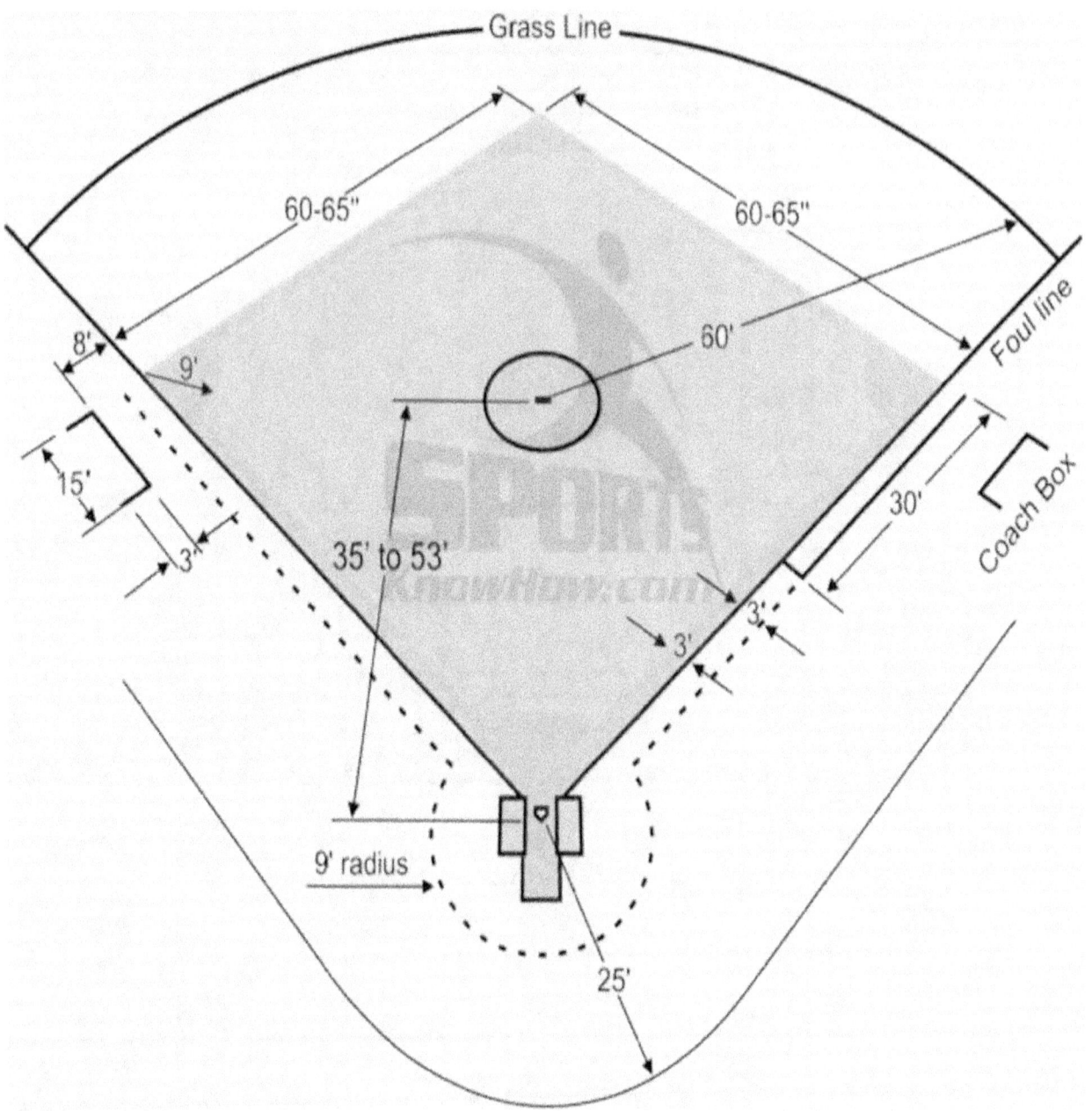

Tennis Court Dimensions

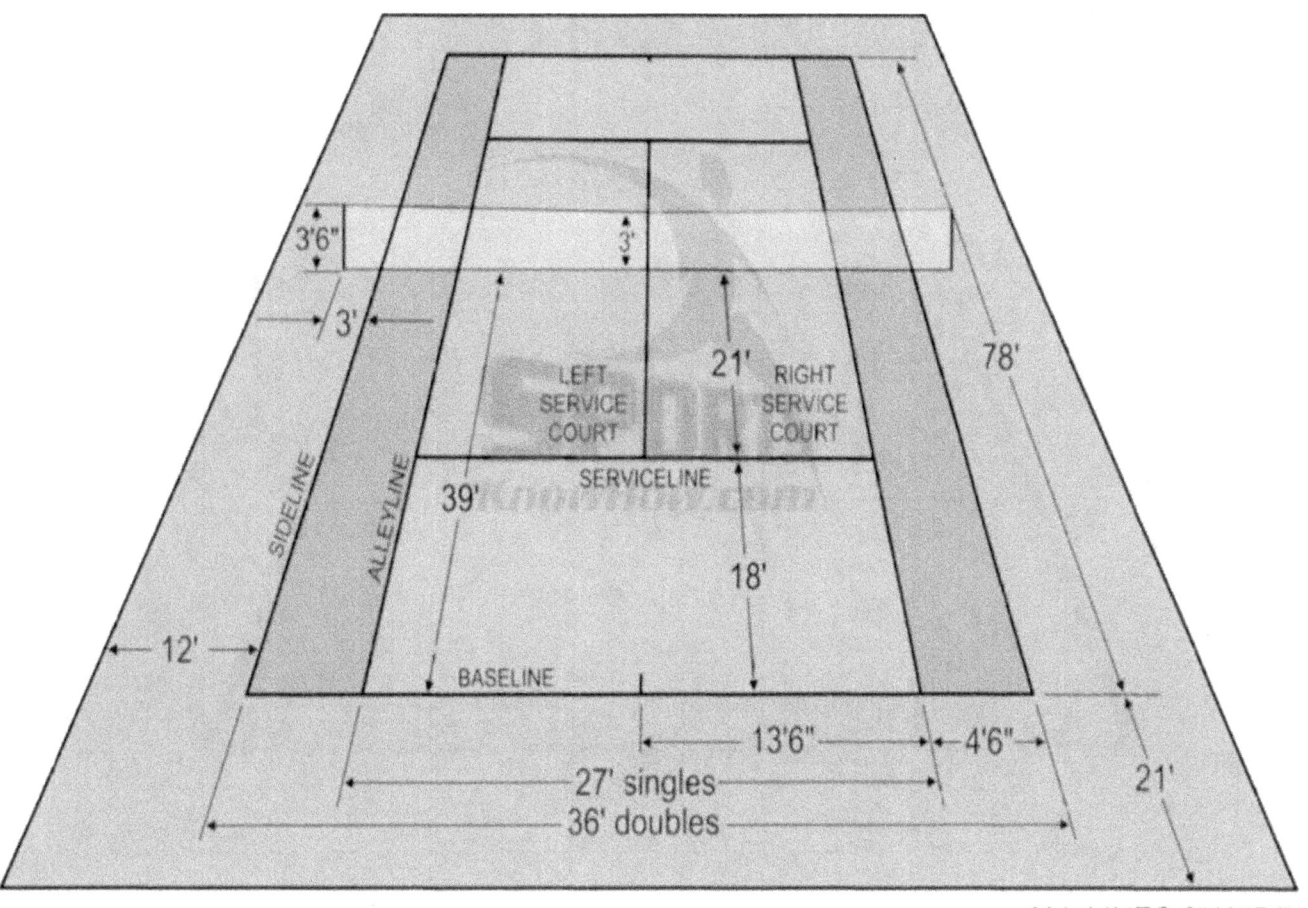

Volleyball Court Dimensions

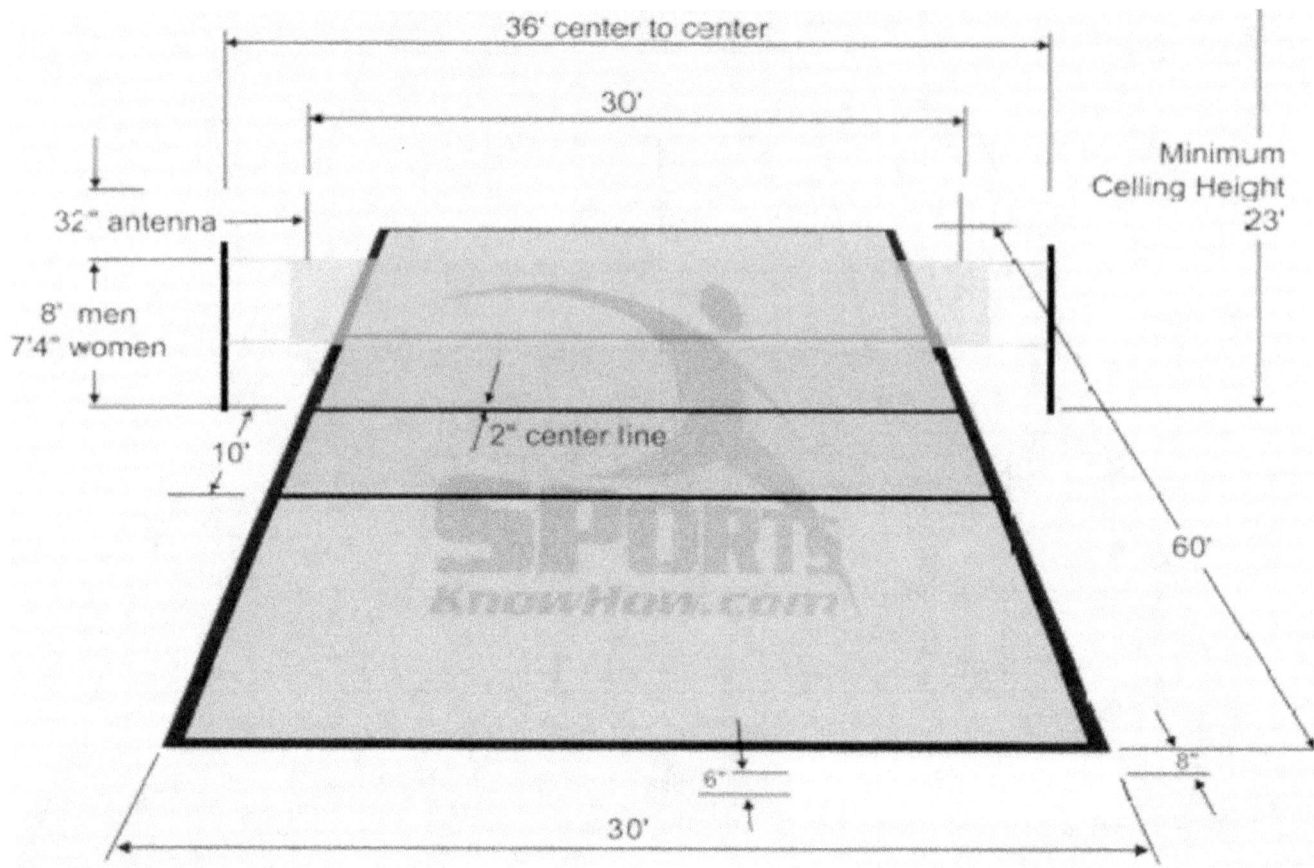

Appendix / 115

Water Polo Pool Dimensions

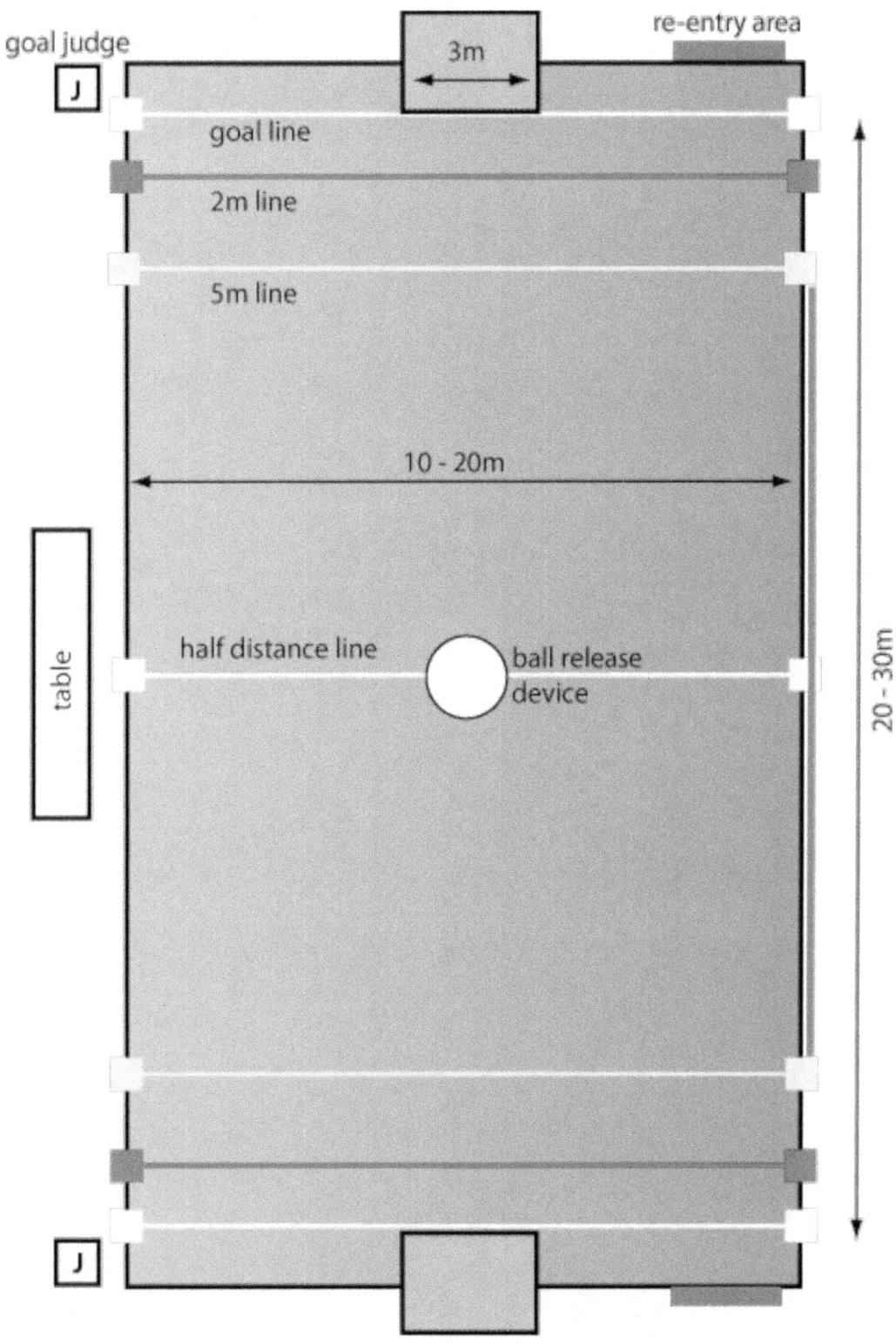

References

Action for Healthy Kids. 2015. "Intramural Program." http://www.actionforhealthykids.org/tools-for-schools/find-challenges/on-the-playground-challenges/1225-intramural-programs.

Anzilotti, Amy. n.d. "Sportsmanship." Accessed January 4, 2019. https://kidshealth.org/en/teens/sportsmanship.html.

Byl, John. 2002. *Intramural Recreation: A Step-by-Step Guide to Creating an Effective Program*. Champaign, IL: Human Kinetics.

California State University Channel Islands. n.d. "Basic Flag Football Rules." Accessed January 28, 2019. https://www.csuci.edu/recreation/basicflagfootballrules.pdf.

Cespedes, Andrea. 2018. "How to Do a Correct Sit-Up." https://www.livestrong.com/article/487008-how-to-do-a-correct-sit-up/.

Hendy, Martin, and Ian McGregor. 1978. *Intramurals: A Teacher's Guide*. New York: Leisure.

IAC Publishing. n.d. "What Are the Rules of High Jump?" Accessed February 2, 2019. https://www.reference.com/sports-active-lifestyle/rules-high-jump-aff6bdd0e0b1bd93.

Kenney, Ian. n.d. "How to Play Frisbee Football." Accessed January 29, 2019. https://www.sportsrec.com/232339-how-to-play-frisbee-football.html.

Lee, Jimson. 2009. "40-Yard Dash Set Up: NFL Scouting Combine Preparation." http://speedendurance.com/2009/12/07/40-yard-dash-set-up-nfl-scouting-combine-preparation/.

Marciano, Fahmei. 2014. "Standing Broad Jump." YouTube video, 0:59. https://www.youtube.com/watch?v=hSunks_4wIE.

McLean Youth Basketball. n.d. "MYB Scorer's and Timekeeper's Responsibilities." Accessed January 7, 2019. http://mcleanbasketball.com/Page.asp?n=31450&org=mcleanbasketball.com.

Montgomery County Public Schools. n.d. "Intramural Sports Program." Accessed January 4, 2019. https://www.montgomeryschoolsmd.org/curriculum/physed/intramural/.

Moss, Dick. n.d. "Intramurals: Slam Dunk Basketball Tournament." Accessed January 18, 2019. https://www.physicaleducationupdate.com/public/405.cfm.

National Intramural Recreational Sports Association. 2012. *Campus Recreational Sports: Managing Employees, Programs, Facilities, and Services*. Champaign, IL: Human Kinetics.

NerdFitness. n.d. "Proper Push-Up Ultimate Guide: How to Do Push Ups with Correct Form." Accessed January 24, 2019. https://www.nerdfitness.com/blog/proper-push-up/.

The New PE. n.d. "Guidelines for School Intramural Programs: A Position Paper from the National Intramural Sports Council." Accessed January 4, 2019. http://www.thenewpe.com/oa/Lecture%20Materials/Topic%2011-Intramurals/Guidelines%20for%20a%20Intramural%20Program.pdf.

Northeast Minor Hockey Association. n.d. "Timekeepers/Official Scorer Responsibilities." Accessed January 7, 2019. https://s3.amazonaws.com/my.llfiles.com/00029734/NEMHA-Timekeeper-Official-Scorer-Responsibilities.pdf.

Northern Secondary School. n.d. "Soccer." Accessed February 2, 2019. http://northern-secondary.com/Joomla/attachments/159_Soccer.pdf.

Print Your Brackets. n.d. "Double Elimination Tournament Brackets." Accessed January 6, 2019. https://www.printyourbrackets.com/double-elimination-tournament-brackets.html.

Print Your Brackets. n.d. "Round Robin Tournament Brackets." Accessed January 6, 2019. https://www.printyourbrackets.com/roundrobin.html.

Print Your Brackets. n.d. "Single Elimination Tournament Brackets." Accessed January 6, 2019. https://www.printyourbrackets.com/single-elimination-tournament-brackets.html.

Quinn, Elizabeth. n.d. "How to Perform the Sit and Reach Flexibility Test." Accessed January 24, 2019. https://www.verywellfit.com/sit-and-reach-flexibility-test-3120279.

Rosenbaum, Mike. n.d. "Illustrated Long Jump Technique." Accessed January 22, 2019. https://www.thoughtco.com/step-by-step-long-jump-technique-3258964.

Rules of Sport. n.d. "Tennis Rules." Accessed February 2, 2019. http://www.rulesofsport.com/sports/tennis.html.

Schaferhoff, Nick. 2015. "9 Effective Marketing Ideas for Sports Teams and Sporting Events." https://www.themeboy.com/blog/9-effective-marketing-ideas-sports-teams-sporting-events/.

Schleyer, Claudia. n.d. "How to Play Flag Football, Part 1: Basic Flag Football Rules." Accessed January 27, 2019. http://www.kids-sports-activities.com/how-to-play-flag-football.html.

Speaks, Laura. 2019. "How to Organize a Cross Country Meet." https://howtheyplay.com/misc/How-to-Organize-a-Cross-Country-Meet.

Sports Know How. n.d. "Court & Field Dimensions Diagram—Homepage." Accessed January 16, 2019. https://www.sportsknowhow.com/dimensions/index.html.

SportsRec. n.d. "How to Do the Shuttle Runs." Accessed January 24, 2019. https://www.sportsrec.com/do-shuttle-runs-4473945.html.

Team New York Aquatics. 2014. "A Beginner's Guide to Water Polo." https://www.tnya.org/wp-content/uploads/2014/07/Polo_Beginners.pdf.

Tennis Tips. n.d. "Doubles Tennis Rules." Accessed February 2, 2019. https://www.tennistips.org/doubles-tennis.html.

Tutorials Point. n.d. "Discus Throw—The Rules." Accessed February 2, 2019. https://www.tutorialspoint.com/discus_throw/discus_throw_rules.htm.

Voleytastic. n.d. "Basic Volleyball Rules." Accessed February 2, 2019. http://www.voleytastic.com/playing-volleyball/basic-volleyball-rules/.

wikiHow. n.d. "How to Build an Obstacle Course." Accessed January 31, 2019. https://www.wikihow.com/Build-an-Obstacle-Course.

wikiHow. n.d. "How to Do Pullups." Accessed January 24, 2019. https://www.wikihow.com/Do-Pullups.

wikiHow. n.d. "How to Long Jump." Accessed January 22, 2019. https://www.wikihow.com/Long-Jump.

wikiHow. n.d. "How to Play Table Tennis/Ping Pong." Accessed February 2, 2019. https://www.wikihow.com/Play-Ping-Pong-(Table-Tennis).

wikiHow. n.d. "How to Shot Put." Accessed February 2, 2019. https://www.wikihow.com/Shot-Put.

Winans, Kerry. n.d. "How to Play around the World Basketball." Accessed January 18, 2019. https://howtoadult.com/play-around-world-basketball-5123080.html.

Zakrajsek, Dorothy B., Lois A. Carnes, and Frank E. Pettigrew Jr. 2003. *Quality Lesson Plans in Secondary Physical Education*, 2nd ed. Champaign, IL: Human Kinetics.

About the Author

University of San Francisco graduate and author **Dr. Kristine Setting Clark** was a longtime feature writer for the San Francisco 49ers' and Dallas Cowboys' *Gameday* magazine. A gifted athlete in her own right, physical education teacher, wife, mother, and, later, a high school administrator and college professor, Dr. Clark has never let anything stand in the way of her goals—not even a life-threatening bout with Hodgkin's disease, blindness in both eyes for 10 months, and the resulting partial blindness at age 26. Her passion for life, her incredible optimism, and her drive to live life to the fullest has endeared her to her former students, friends, and those on whom she's written, including her childhood football idol and close friend Bob St. Clair of the San Francisco 49ers.

Besides *Undefeated, Untied, and Uninvited: A Documentary of the 1951 University of San Francisco Dons' Football Team*, she has authored nine other books, including *Legends of the Hall: 1950s, St Clair: I'll Take It Raw: The Life of Former San Francisco 49er and Hall of Fame Member Bob St. Clair, Lilly: A Cowboy's Story—The Life of Former Dallas Cowboys and Hall of Fame Member Bob Lilly, Tittle: Nothing Comes Easy—The Life of Former Football Great and Hall of Fame Member Y. A. Tittle, The Fire Within—The Life of Former Green Bay Packer and Hall of Fame Member Jim Taylor*, and *Controlled Violence—The Life of Former New York Giant, Washington Redskins and Hall of Fame Member Sam Huff*.

Released in July 2014 was the book *The Fighting Donovans—A Family History of World Boxing Champion and Hall of Fame Boxer Mike Donovan, World Champion Boxing Referee and Boxing Hall of Fame Referee Arthur Donovan, Sr. and Former Baltimore Colt Defensive Tackle and Pro Football Hall of Fame Member Arthur Donovan, Jr.* In September 2015, her book *Cheating Is Encouraged!* with former Raider tight end Mike Siani was released through Skyhorse Publishing (an imprint of W. W. Norton in New York), and in March 2016, her book titled *Football's Fabulous Fifties—When Men Were Men and the Grass Was Still Real* was released.

In March 2016, her *Simply English* 3 book curriculum for ESL and special education students was published by Rowman & Littlefield.

Over the years, she has held a number of book signing events with the many celebrities from her books at the Pro Football Hall of Fame in Canton, Ohio. She has also been a keynote speaker for many corporate, sports, and educational venues.

Dr. Clark's personality, close relationships with the subjects of her books, and engaging writing style allow her to reach the subject matter on a deeper level, taking the reader to otherwise unavailable territory: the sometimes humorous, always intriguing backstories of the famous events and players in the world of sports. In addition, her achievements have led to an offer to host a sports talk radio show and invitations as a keynote speaker for many corporate, sports, and educational venues.

In 1977, Clark was diagnosed with Stage IV Hodgkin's disease and was given three months to live. She eventually beat the disease after enduring 10 months of blindness caused by the grueling chemotherapy treatments. In December 2015, she wrote her memoir titled *Death Was Never an Option! A Hu-*

morously Serious Story on Defeating Cancer and Blindness. The television treatment was written by Jamie Williams, former San Francisco 49er tight end and screenwriter of the movie *Any Given Sunday*.

Dr. Clark resides in Stockton, California, and has two grown children and four grandsons. Her oldest grandson, Justin, is the godson of former All-Pro 49er and Hall of Fame member Bob St. Clair.

www.ingramcontent.com/pod-product-compliance
Lightning Source LLC
Chambersburg PA
CBHW082206230426
43672CB00015B/2919